SO-DUL-255

AN OUTLINE AND MANUAL
OF LOGIC

AN OUTLINE AND MANUAL
OF LOGIC

By JOSEPH McLAUGHLIN, S.J.

MARQUETTE UNIVERSITY

REVISED EDITION

MILWAUKEE

MARQUETTE UNIVERSITY PRESS

1938

DOMINICAN COLLEGE
LIBRARY
SAN RAFAEL

160
M222

Copyright, 1932
MARQUETTE UNIVERSITY PRESS
MILWAUKEE, WISCONSIN
U. S. A.

62646

Printed in United States of America

A more ambitious, because a more comprehensive contrivance still, for interpreting the concrete world is the method of logical inference. What we desiderate is something which may supersede the need of personal gifts by a far reaching and infallible rule. Now, without external symbols to mark out and to study its course, the intellect runs wild; but with the aid of symbols, as in algebra, it advances with precision and effect. Let then our symbols be words; let all thought be arrested and embodied in words. Let language have a monopoly of thought; and thought go for only so much as it can show itself to be worth in language. Let every prompting of the intellect be ignored, every momentum of argument be disowned, which is unprovided with an equivalent wording, as its ticket for sharing in the common search after truth. Let the authority of nature, common-sense, experience, genius, go for nothing. Ratiocination, thus restricted and put into grooves, is what I have called 'Inference,' and the science, which is its regulating principle, is LOGIC. (Cardinal Newman, *A Grammar of Assent*, pp. 262-263.)

PREFACE

The following twelve chapters of Logic were put together from some notes gathered by the writer, from time to time, while he was engaged in teaching the subject.

The book is intended to be a practical text and manual for beginners; in particular, for that class of college students whose curriculum of studies allots to them for the study of Logic only three semester hours for one semester.

Even more specifically,—while preparing this Outline and Manual,—the writer had in mind that special class of beginners in Logic who are known, nowadays, in the colleges as 'pre-students' of some kind or other; pre-medics, pre-legals and so on.

Because of the limited opportunity 'pre-students' have for a more adequate course in philosophy, it seemed to the writer that they especially, needed to be taught in a very particular way, to appreciate the value and the practical use of Logic more than to be trained to a masterly academic knowledge of it.

At the same time, it will hardly be considered poor pedagogy to stress the practical aspect of the science in point, with those students for whom Logic is to be the beginning of a complete and thorough course in philosophy. After all, students who intend to take a complete course of philosophy while in college, not otherwise than pre-students,—cannot be expected to grasp the finer academic points and niceties of Logic with only a short formal course in the subject for one semester. A sensitive dialectical mind is the fruit, it would seem, of much experience with other parts of philosophy, especially Metaphysics,—acquired long after the formal course in Logic is finished.

Accordingly, on account of the purpose of this book,—to teach the use of Logic rather than to give a purely scholastic knowledge of it,—this Outline and Manual will undoubtedly give evidence of limitations which might not be tolerated in a more adequate text or in one intended to be a scholarly contribution to the age-old science which Aristotle has left us.

It will be noted that in accordance with its particular purpose, the book makes much of the principle: "Per exempla discimus." No originality can be claimed for this. It is referred to here, just because, in accordance with the purpose of the book, it seems to be as important that both teachers and students give the same, if not more assiduous attention to the examples of good and bad Logic in the book as to the study of the text itself.

Finally, in preparing this Outline and Manual, a very free use of other texts of Logic has been made. To check up recognition for these texts in every instance would be an impossible task. But happily, it does not seem that this impossible task is ethically necessary, since the book is not intended to be scholarly or original, and since where the writer may express himself as others do, the subject matter is objectively fixed and the mode of expression, more or less stereotyped. A similar reason may be advanced for the absence of an apology for the appropriation of many of the book's examples of good and bad Logic from the pages of other text books. Most of them are common enough to be considered as belonging to a sort of general clearing house for any prospective publication on The Art and Science of Reasoning.

For most of the material on Validity-vs-Truth, however, special recognition seems rightfully due to Dotterer's Beginners' Logic. In no other text did the writer find this question so satisfactorily or so forcibly treated. It is with Mr. Dotterer's kind permission therefore, that the present writer has embodied the exposition of Validity-vs-Truth in the pages of this text, substantially as it is in Beginners' Logic.

To the Reverend Michael Mahoney, author of Essentials of Formal Logic, the writer likewise wishes to express his thanks for permission to reprint his treatment of the subject of Induction as Chapter Twelve of the present text, almost in the same way as Fr. Mahoney has it in Essentials of Formal Logic.

Lastly, in addition to the recognition just given to Mr. Dotterer and to Fr. Mahoney, the writer wishes to express, 'in globo,' his indebtedness to the Logic texts of: Clarke, Coffey, Creighton, Mercier, Poland, Sellars, Shallo, Sortais, and Turner.

J. McL.

CONTENTS

CONTENTS

CONTENTS

CONTENTS

CONTENTS

AN OUTLINE AND MANUAL
OF LOGIC

AN OUTLINE AND MANUAL OF LOGIC

CHAPTER I

INTRODUCTION

Logic Is Straight Thinking.—A clever Irish lad once defined Logic nicely and concisely when he said: "Logic is straight thinking." When we study Logic, the burden of our efforts is just that:—Logic is a study of the rules for straight thinking.

What is Straight Thinking?—Straight thinking is thinking so controlled and disciplined that it will exclude from the process of our thought all inconsistency and all implicit or explicit contradiction in our concepts or ideas.

Straight thinking does not necessarily guarantee us objective truth. On the other hand, without straight thinking, we can never attain objective truth.

When our thinking is straight, it is said to be valid. Our thinking has a truth value only when it corresponds to reality distinct from us as the subjects thinking.

Very often we distort reality when we think. This we do either because we erroneously interpret our thoughts as presenting to our mind realities which do not exist at all, or because we read into our concepts or ideas more reality or less reality than our concepts or ideas, in any specific instance, represent to our mind. Finally, we often mistake the kind of reality that is represented to our minds by our concepts or ideas.

It may be said that the general aim of the Science of Logic is to teach us how to measure exactly the correspondence that arises between the mind and reality distinct from the mind, when we think. How it does guide us in measuring exactly this correspondence between the mind and reality distinct from the mind, will be appreciated after the principles and rules of the science shall have been mastered.

The Father of Logic.—Aristotle, the famous Greek Philosopher, is rightly considered to be the Father of Logic. It was he who left us the science complete and systematized. So complete indeed, was Aristotle's work on Logic, that with but little additional content, the principles and rules of the science have remained substantially the same since his time. That the Stagirite formulated the principles and rules of Logic means that by analyzing how men validly thought, he established the norms according to which we must guide our thinking if we would effectively marshal the cognitional acts of the mind when we think, and thus introduce that order into them without which they would never lead us to truth.

Natural Logic.—Men formed judgments consistently and they reasoned rightly, it is true, before Aristotle ever laid down a rule of Logic. In fact, whenever anyone thinks or forms a judgment; whenever anyone makes an inference or performs an act of reasoning according to the dictate of his rational nature; he is making use of Logic, of a sort of natural Logic, of which no sane man is entirely destitute.

Common Sense.—We are accustomed to call the thinking we do, the judgments we formulate, and the reasoning processes we go through according to this dictate of our rational nature;—'acting according to common sense.' But common sense is of itself far from infallible; it really does not carry us very far or very safely beyond any but simple and easy deductions or inferences. In difficult matters of thought, of judgment, or of reasoning, we must needs pause and reflect maturely on all the circumstances of any particular problem of thought before us; we must review and analyze the circumstances of our thought-problem; and then, very often, if not nearly always, our experience will be that we shall have to reconstruct our thinking more carefully, either in part or as a whole, if we wish to eliminate error from it completely. Is it not a fact that even shrewd, clever people, often find out that their spontaneous judgments have misled them?

A Formal Study of Logic Necessary.—True it is, that just as in the time before Aristotle, so even at the present day, it is quite possible to pick up by imitation or perhaps by inheritance, the correct way of orderly thinking without giving any attention to the study of Logic, in the same way that it is possible for a person who has been extremely fortunate in his early associations,—in those whose speech he has heard or in the books which he had read,—to speak and write correctly, without knowing anything about grammar as it is studied in the schools. Most people, however, have not been so fortunate. Little observation of the oral or written speech of men is required to convince us that neither the habit of grammatical expression nor that of logical thinking is very widespread.

Why We Study Logic.—Accordingly, we study Logic to familiarize ourselves with the established principles and rules to which correct thinking processes must conform if we wish to avoid the innumerable pitfalls and fallacies to which such processes are commonly exposed. We study Logic to learn how to think and reason always, but especially in difficult matters, with clearness and consistency, or without contradicting ourselves. We study Logic to learn how to be exact in interpreting and expressing the thoughts which happen to come to our minds as well as those which we consciously develop in our mind.

What Logic Will Do for Us.—It must be understood that Logic does not profess to guard us infallibly against error in our processes of thought or in the oral or written expression of it. What Logic will do for us particularly, however, is this: it will develop in us a worth while habit of detecting error in much that we read or hear, with the consequent likelihood that we shall avoid error in our own processes of thought as well as in the oral or written expression of our thought. Of one who has acquired the habit of logical thinking, it will at least be safe so to say that he will be alert of mind, and sanely cautious about not accepting what is apparent, for real truth. We might add also that, as a general rule, one who has acquired the habit of logical thinking, will

hardly be rash or too foolhardy in disseminating coun-
terfeit for real logical truth.

A Practical Science.—It is quite obvious that Logic
is a practical science. Of all the practical and specula-
tive sciences, Logic in a sense, is pre-eminent. No matter what other sciences we might wish to learn; without
Logic, our efforts to learn them would be in vain, because Logic must regulate the content of every science.
All of them must be drawn up according to Logic's
laws. It is in this sense, in particular, that Logic leads
us to truth.

Logic—A Science and an Art.—Logic is both a
science and an art. That systematically established body
of principles and rules which must be adhered to, in
order to think clearly and consistently is called the
science of Logic. Such a familiar knowledge of the
principles and rules of Logic which will guarantee an
habitual use of them with facility by anyone when he
thinks, is what is meant by the art of Logic.

The Utility of Logic.—The utility of Logic, therefore, is seen above all, from the fact that the science
and the art of Logic taken together, will assure us of
thinking consistently, and of thus rewarding us with
that right temperament of mind which must be pre-
supposed as conditional for the attainment of truth.
This fact alone is reason enough why Logic is of such
indispensable value as an introduction to philosophy.

Mental Sloth.—The study and mastery of the principles and rules of Logic is of prime importance also,

for the very special psychological reason that we need just that peculiar discipline of mind which the study and mastering of Logic affords, in order to overcome the habit of mental sloth to which most men are addicted. It is so much easier to imagine than to search; —so much simpler to guess than to prove;—so much more pleasing to see what we wish to see than what really is;—so much more natural to yield to a prejudice than to curb it. If Logic does not profess to lead us directly to truth, at least it patrols and controls the avenues which do lead thereto. Indeed, Logic stands out for all time as 'THE KEEPER OF THE TEMPLE OF TRUTH.' Like a faithful watchman, Logic warns us,— among other dangers on the way to THE TEMPLE OF TRUTH,—of myths and the myth-making faculty of men; of unwarranted and false assumptions; of pseudo conclusions which do not necessarily follow from premises stated or implied. Logic warns us also against credulity, inadequate tests, faults of language and the trickery of words. In fine, Logic both warns and safeguards us against the innumerable pitfalls and fallacies of our thought-processes of every kind as well as against the inexact expression of our thought itself.

SOME NOTES ON LOGIC FOR BEGINNERS

It is futile for anyone to attempt criticizing an instance of oral or written speech for its logic or its lack of it, before he is certain that he understands clearly and exactly what the speaker is saying or what statements or propositions the writer is presenting to him through the written word.

This prerequisite just referred to, obviously implies, in turn, an easy familiarity with the grammatical and idiomatic structure of the language in which one is reading or to which he is listening.

We should begin our critical analysis of a speaker's or writer's statements or propositions with this initial attitude of mind: we should be convinced that no man's statements or propositions are worth any more than the proof he can offer in support of his statements or propositions if these are not immediately evident.

Moreover, even the proof offered by a speaker or writer in support of his statements or propositions may not prove. For this reason a student of Logic must not only not assent spontaneously to any statements or propositions which he reads or hears, when they are not objectively and immediately evident, but he must likewise subject to a critical examination the proof which a speaker or writer offers in support of his statements or propositions.

Statements or propositions, not objectively and immediately evident, are rarely proposed to us for our acceptance or belief, in simple categorical form, e.g., This is a good aeroplane. On the contrary, a speaker or writer almost always instinctively offers us some kind of a proof in support of the propositions or statements which he makes, if his propositions or statements are not cogent enough to compel our assent to them.

When the proof of a statement or proposition takes the form of a subordinate clause in a grammatically complex sentence, students of Logic do not find it especially difficult to distinguish the given statement or proposition from the proof offered in support of the statement or proposition, e.g., This man is intoxicated because he walks with an unsteady gait.

When, however, a speaker's or writer's statement or proposition together with the proof of the statement or proposition, are presented in the form of two or more grammatically independent sentences, the tyro in Logic very often finds it difficult to determine which is the speaker's or writer's statement or proposition and which is his proof.

In the following argument, for instance, what is the writer trying to make his readers assent to, and what is the proof that he offers for his contention? Alcoholic liquor has been the ruin of many a family. Who then will criticize our prohibition laws? (*See Note).

Sometimes what the speaker or writer wishes us to assent to or believe, is not set forth at all by any of his words. This means that his statement or proposition is implied in the proposition or statement which he does present to us, and that it must be inferred by the reader or hearer himself. For instance, what did Shakespeare mean to tell us when in Julius Caesar he wrote: "Yon Cassius has a mean and hungry look. Such men are dangerous."?

Students of Logic must learn to read what is set before them on the written or printed page. This means that they must learn not to read into a statement or proposition, what the statement or proposition does not say. To be sure, this rule does not imply that it is illogical to change what we read or hear, into other equiva-

---

*NOTE: Oratorical questions must be turned into direct statements or into direct propositions in any logical discussion. The science does not deal with or recognize oratorical questions as such.

lent words: the important thing is not to change the idea or meaning of what is verbally or orally presented to us.

In particular, students of Logic must not change affirmative statements or propositions presented to them for criticism or discussion, into the negative form of these statements or propositions.

Secondly, students of Logic must guard against changing into the passive voice construction, any statement or proposition presented to them as constructed with the active voice of the verb.

In a word, a student of Logic must be careful to criticize or discuss any statement or proposition presented to him, exactly as it is presented. A logician is not concerned about criticizing or discussing what might be in the speaker's or writer's mind in any particular instance, but only about the logic or the lack of it in the speaker's or writer's written or oral speech.

Finally, let the student be sparing in the use of the personal pronoun, "it." Whenever the student is tempted to use this pronoun, he would do well to ask himself: What do I mean by the word, "it," in my present use of the word? After asking this question, he will see, nine times out of ten, that the noun which the pronoun "it" is intended to signify, would express his idea much more clearly and forcibly.

QUESTIONS FOR A REVIEW OF CHAPTER I

1. What is straight thinking?
2. When is our thinking valid?
3. When has our thinking truth value?
4. How do we often distort reality when we think?
5. What may be said to be the general aim of Logic?
6. What does the science of Logic owe to Aristotle?

7. What is natural Logic? Why is it not sufficient for effective thinking?
8. If the study of Logic will not guard us infallibly against error in our thinking, what is the use of studying it?
9. For what reason is Logic pre-eminent among the sciences?
10. Explain the difference between the science and the art of Logic.
11. How will the study of Logic help to curb our mental sloth?
12. Give a summary of the precautions set down on Page 6 for beginners in Logic.

MATERIAL FOR THEME WORK SUGGESTED BY THE CONTENT OF CHAPTER I

1. I feel sure I made an 'A' in today's quiz.
2. I don't see why I received a 'D' in Mathematics. I studied it so hard.
3. Jane said she just knew she would never get a square deal from Prof. X.
4. Automobiles kill hundreds every day. They ought to be done away with.
5. God is too good to punish with hell-fire.*
6. "The fool hath said in his heart, 'there is no God'."
7. "Pilate said to the Jews: 'I find no cause in Him . . . I will chastise Him, therefore, and let Him go'."
8. If the hypothesis of God works satisfactorily, in the widest sense of the term, it is true. (W. James, *Pragmatism*, p. 229.)
9. Alcoholic liquor has been the ruin of many a family. Who then will criticize our Prohibition Laws?
10. That there was a dawn of moral consciousness in the human race is certain. We assume that there must have been a time in history of the Human Race when men

---

* Express statement and proof in two sentences.

were non-moral. This assumption cannot be directly proved for we know of no human beings who have no ideas of ethical practice. (Blackmar and Gillen, *Outline of Sociology*, p. 222.)

11. The first scraps of this skull were found in an excavation for road gravel in Sussex. Bit by bit other fragments of this skull were hunted out from the quarry heaps until most of it could be pieced together. It is a thick skull, thicker than that of any living race of men and it has a brain capacity intermediate between the pithecanthropus and men. (H. G. Wells, *Outline of History*, Ch. I.)

12. Philosophy begins where one learns to doubt, particularly one's cherished beliefs,—one's dogmas, and one's axioms. (Will Durant, *The Story of Philosophy*, p. 12.)

13. Scientists are certain that men have lived in Europe more than twenty times as long as the world period of written history. . . . Of all the outward marks that distinguish man from the animals, probably the use of fire is the earliest and for long ages it was the most important. . . . Scientists believe it (*human speech*) came as a slow evolution from sounds or actions such as animals use in expressing feelings or in giving warning to one another. . . . A belief in life after death . . . is found in some early religions. . . . On the other hand, there rarely existed in primitive religions a belief that the future holds a place of rewards or punishments for the acts of this life. (McKinley, Howland-Dann., *World History in the making*, Ch. I.)

14. Education has for its chief function the development of the individual in such wise that life may yield the greatest amount of joy and happiness to him and through him to the social group in which he lives.

15. Religion is therefore to be regarded as a product of inner growth, a natural result of the stages of feeling through which man passes. Religion has its sanction within us, and all religious ceremonies are valuable only as they introduce the individual to powers within himself that are unexpressed. The higher truths of religion are revelation to a single self from the racial or cosmic self within his. . . . (Partridge, *Genetic Philosophy of Education*, p. 56.)

Some important statements made throughout the foregoing paragraphs of Ch. I, which should be made use of in developing a critical exposition of the false logic or the absolute lack of all logic that characterizes the 'Material for Theme Work,' as presented above.

1. *We must needs pause and reflect maturely on all the circumstances of any thought problem.* Does the writer seem to have done so in this particular statement or paragraph which you have under consideration?
2. *Even shrewd, clever people, often find out that their SPONTANEOUS judgments have misled them.* Perhaps this particular statement, proposition or argument which you are criticizing, smacks of a spontaneous judgment?
3. *We study Logic to learn how to think and reason always . . . with clearness and consistency, or without contradicting ourselves.* Does the writer's present statement, proposition or argument show any lack of clearness of expression? any inconsistency? any contradictions in ideas?
4. *We study Logic to learn how to be exact in interpreting and expressing the thoughts which happen to come to our minds as well as those which we consciously develop in our mind.* Does the writer whose statements you are examining, seem to be falsely interpreting the thought in his mind? Is he inexact in the expression of his thought?

5. *Of one who has acquired the habit of logical thinking, it will be safe to say . . . that he will be sanely cautious about not accepting APPARENT for REAL truth.* In what you are criticizing is there any apparent but not real truth?

6. *It is so much EASIER to IMAGINE than to search.* Is the writer of what you are criticizing guilty of this bad habit?

7. *. . . so much simpler to GUESS than to PROVE.* What about the writer of what you are now criticizing? Does he seem to be guessing, not proving?

8. *. . . so much more pleasing to see WHAT WE WISH TO SEE than what really is.* Any evidence of this in the proposition or statement before you?

9. *. . . so much natural to YIELD TO A PREJUDICE THAN TO CURB IT.* Perhaps that is just what your writer is guilty of. Can we ever come to truth by way of FEELING or EMOTION, or isn't it only through REASON?

10. *Logic warns us of . . . UNWARRANTED, of FALSE ASSUMPTIONS, of PSEUDO CONCLUSIONS which do not NECESSARILY follow from premises stated or implied.* May it not be that the paragraph you are concerned with is just reeking with this kind of false logic?

11. *Logic warns us against CREDULITY, INADEQUATE TESTS, FAULTS OF LANGUAGE, TRICKERY OF WORDS.* Are you guilty of believing without reflection, anything and everything you read or hear—i.e., things, which are not immediately evident? Any evidence that the writer of what you are criticizing has not ADEQUATELY tested the contention or the point of what he says? Any incoherent expressions in what he writes? Does he express himself not only grammatically but in accordance with the three fundamental essentials of good rhetoric—UNITY, COHERENCE and FORCE?

Suggestions which may be useful in preparing an outline for themes on the statements, propositions or paragraphs proposed for critical theme work on pages 10, 11 and 12.

When criticizing one statement or proposition with one or more proofs:

1.   Distinguish between the writer's statement or proposition and the proof which he offers in support of his statement or proposition.

2.   Discuss the value of the proof offered. A proof offered in support of a statement or proposition does not prove, unless the statement or proposition necessarily follows from the proof.

3.   Possible reasons why the proof offered by the writer in support of his statement or proposition are worthless may be found among those statements restated on pages 12 and 13 from the preceding pages of this Chapter I. Consider how one or more of these statements may now be applied in your theme.

When writing a critical theme on a paragraph:

1.   Indicate the topic sentence of the paragraph. If topic sentence is not expressed, state in your own words what it is supposed to be.

2.   Discuss whether the other sentences of the paragraph add any support to the statement in the topic sentence.

3.   Discuss the logic or the lack of it in each sentence taken separately.

Note: A number of sentences strung together do not necessarily make a paragraph in the rhetorical or logical sense. Be certain that what you are criticizing is a valid paragraph before you begin your theme.

Note: It is not intended that Chapter One should be mastered perfectly by the student before he proceeds to the detailed and formal study of Logic in the succeeding chapters. It is not the purpose of Chapter One to teach the student any of the rules of Logic in a formal way but to provoke or stir up his mind to an appreciation of the logical way of thinking.

Some may find it to be better method not to start off the course in Logic with Chapter One or at least not to delay upon it in a formal way, but only to refer to it from time to time after the student has learned the more important principles and rules of the science.

CHAPTER II

SOME PRELIMINARY NOTIONS AND DEFINITIONS

What Is Logic?—Logic is the science which deals with the correct processes of thinking, i.e., it is that systematic body of scientifically established principles and rules which must be adhered to, in order to secure straight or consistent thought in those operations of the mind by which all our knowledge is acquired.

The Cognitive Acts of the Mind.—The acts or operations of the mind through which all our knowledge is acquired are three in number:—simple apprehension; —judgment;—and inference or reasoning.

Simple Apprehension.—Simple apprehension is that act or operation of the mind by which the mind merely conforms itself to any objective reality distinct from the mind without affirming or denying anything about it.

Idea or Concept.—The product of the act of simple apprehension is called an idea or concept. Specifically, an idea or a concept is the representation in the mind of any real object—(possible or actual; material, immaterial or spiritual)—distinct from the mind as the subject thinking.*

---

* The mind may have *itself* for the object of its thought, but even in this case the *mind* as object is distinguished from the mind as the subject thinking. In like manner 'beings of the mind' are distinct from the mind as the subject thinking.

Terms.—The oral or written expression of an idea or the object of an idea is called a term. A term may be only one word or it may consist of a group of words which have to be taken together in order to be capable of expressing an idea, e.g., boy, man, the boys in blue, the men of the 20th Century.

In a simple categorical proposition, there can be two and only two terms, the subject term and the predicate term. The logical copula—(is, am, are)—must never be considered as a term. The subject term is all the words that precede the copula, taken as a unit. The predicate term of a proposition is all the words that follow the copula taken as a unit.

Judgment.—Judgment is that act of the mind by which we affirm or deny the identity between the objects of two ideas. The oral or written expression of a judgment is called a proposition. Specifically, a proposition is the oral or written expression of any statement;—any affirmation or denial, by means of the verb 'to be' in the present tense, indicative mood; in any of the three persons, and in either the singular or plural number, e.g., Honesty is the best policy.

Inference or Reasoning.—The third act or operation of the mind by which we think and can acquire knowledge, called inference or reasoning;—is of two kinds:—immediate and mediate.

Immediate Inference.—Immediate inference is that act or operation of the mind by which we bring out explicitly in a second proposition, a judgment which was implicitly contained in another given proposition; e.g., No man is an angel; therefore, no angel is a man.

Mediate Inference.—Mediate inference is that act or operation of the mind by which we bring out explicitly in a third proposition or in any number of successive propositions thereafter, any new judgment which was implicitly contained in the relationship between two or more antecedent propositions stated or implied.

Example of Mediate Inference.—All men are mortal; John is a man;—therefore, John is mortal. Mortals are beings who will die; therefore, John is one who will die. But, all who die will be happy or miserable for all eternity; therefore, John will be happy or miserable for all eternity.

The Aim of Logic.—Logic is the science which deals with the correct processes of thought. As thought in general, consists of the representation in the mind of some reality distinct from the mind, and as there are three operations of the mind by which we think; the aim or purpose of Logic is threefold:—First, Logic aims to teach us how to measure exactly the degree of representation in the mind there happens to be in any particular concept whenever the object of the concept is expressed orally or by a written term;—Secondly, Logic purports to teach us how to form judgments consistently or without contradicting ourselves;—Thirdly, Logic teaches us the rules for making valid inferences, i.e., inferences which follow as necessary consequences from stated or implied premises.

Logic Divided Into Three Parts.—From the foregoing paragraph it is easily seen that the study of Logic
will divide itself broadly into three parts:

1. The Laws of Logic about ideas or concepts together with the Laws of Logic about terms as the oral
or written expressions of our ideas or the objects of our
ideas.

2. The Laws of Logic about judgments, and about
propositions as the oral or written expressions of our
judgments.

3. The Laws of Logic about inference or reasoning together with the Laws of Logic on the various oral
or written expressions which inference and reasoning
can assume, the syllogism, enthymeme, dilemma, and so
on.

Hypothetical Value.—The Laws of Logic have only
an hypothetical value. By this is meant that of themselves, they do not guarantee to assure us of 'objective
logical truth.' They aim only to guide us in our processes of thinking so that we may do our thinking consistently or without contradicting ourselves. Strictly
speaking, the Laws of Logic have nothing to do with
the material content of our thought. Logic does not
primarily attend to the question of whether the material of our concepts, our judgments or our inferences
is objectively true or not. At times, however, the Laws
of Logic, primarily concerned with validity or consistency in our thinking, seem to overlap with the laws for
'objective logical truth.' The fallacy of 'begging the
question,' for instance, arises from the error of basing
an argument on an assumption that is not objectively

true or at least on one which has not been proved to be true. Similarly, the invalidity of any immediate inference according to the method of opposition, is based on the truth or falsehood through quantity and quality of immediately related propositions.

For the present, we need not go too deeply into this question of the overlapping of the laws of validity with the laws for objective truth. Mastering the Laws of Logic as they have been traditionally taught, together with learning a few simple rules for testing the objective truth of the judgments or propositions used in any argument is the goal at which it will be sufficient to aim.

The Truth of Concepts.—Our concepts of themselves always truthfully represent their object. The error in Logic in regard to concepts comes from the false interpretation we give to them as representations of reality. Logic aims to teach us how to measure the degree of representation there happens to be in any concept, as well as to determine just what kind of representation there is in any particular concept when we outwardly give expression to it by means of a term. Logic teaches us this correct interpretation of concepts when it teaches us about the nature of concepts and terms and when it teaches us the value of the different kinds of concepts and terms.

Validity of Judgments. In regard to judgments, Logic is concerned primarily with their validity or consistency. It teaches us that our judgments are valid or consistent, when there is a true, even though an inadequate relation of identity between the reality represented by the subject term of a proposition and that represented by the predicate term of the same proposition;—in brief, when there is no contradiction—apparent or implied—between the subject and predicate of any proposition.

Validity of Inference.—Our inferences are valid only when our conclusions follow from our stated or implied propositions or premises as necessary consequences.

Validity vs. Truth.—The immediate aim of Logic then, is to teach us how to secure straight thinking in our processes of thought; at most, only indirectly will it guarantee to direct us in attaining objective logical truth as well. The question of Logic is primarily one of validity, not one of truth.

It is important that the student beginning the study of Logic should grasp the distinction between the concept of 'validity' and the concept of 'truth.' Not only are 'truth' and 'validity' distinct concepts but neither is an unfailing index of the other. The adjectives: 'true' and 'false' are properly applied to propositions, and then the words imply that the propositions to which they are applied are, or are not trustworthy expressions of some particular reality which does exist objectively, distinct from the mind as the subject thinking.

The terms, 'valid' and 'invalid' are properly applied to arguments or to our processes of thought from concept to judgment, and from judgment to inference or reasoning. The words imply nothing more than that there is no inconsistency or contradiction of thought as we pass from concepts to judgments, or from judgments to newly inferred judgments by our acts of reasoning, in any particular instance.

If an argument is formally correct, i.e., if in combining or relating the object of one concept with that of another, there is no inconsistency or contradiction of thought; or, if in inferring a conclusion from one or more premises we affirm or deny only what necessarily follows or does not follow; our argument or process of thought is valid. If in addition, our premises express objective logical truth, our argument or our process of thought may properly be called 'good,' and our conclusions will then be true as well as valid.

A Good Machine.—A valid argument or a valid process of thought is a good mental machine. If it is fed with good material, i.e., with judgments or propositions which are objectively true, it will yield a satisfactory product. On the other hand, however good the machine may be, if it is fed with inferior material, i.e., with judgments or propositions which are objectively false, the operator has no right to expect anything but an unsatisfactory product, i.e., conclusions which although valid in form, are false as representations of reality.

The Danger of Logic.—Herein,—namely, in the fact that 'validity' and 'truth' are not the same thing,— lies the danger of Logic. Herein lies the reason for that undeserved contempt of the science of Logic which some superficial scholars at times, affect. Herein lies the explanation of the tricks of the ancient Sophists, by which they could make the weaker argument appear the stronger, or the contradictory of any proposition just as plausible as the proposition itself.

The Story of Philosophy.—In our own day, Will Durant writes on page 222 of his phenomenal 'best seller,'—The Story of Philosophy, thus:—"His (Voltaire's) later educators, the Jesuits, gave him the very instrument of Scepticism, by teaching him Dialectic, (Logic), the art of proving anything, and therefore at last, the habit of believing nothing."—If Durant is sincere, this passage would seem to prove that he himself never studied Logic, or if he did, that he never learned what it was all about;—at least, that he failed to appreciate that the Laws of Logic have only a hypothetical value. This in turn, means that he failed to grasp, as every beginner in Logic should grasp,—the distinction between the concepts of 'validity' and 'truth.'

Validity and Truth Continued.—Let the tyro in Logic understand then, that an argument or a process of thought may be valid even though some or all of its component parts may be false. On the other hand, a process of reasoning may be invalid, although all of its component parts may be true.

Consider the following examples:—

No Pennsylvanians are Canadians;
All Philadelphians are Pennsylvanians;
No Philadelphians are Canadians.

Not only is this syllogism valid but all the propositions of which it is composed are objectively true,—both premises and the conclusion.

Suppose that we should substitute for Canadians, the term, 'Americans,' without changing the other terms of the syllogism. We should then have:—

No Pennsylvanians are Americans;
All Philadelphians are Pennsylvanians;
No Philadelphians are Americans.

In this syllogism the first, or the major premise, as well as the conclusion is false. Nevertheless, the syllogism is valid: it violates no rule of the syllogism, as we shall show in a succeeding chapter. Because in this second syllogism, one of the supporting propositions was false, no satisfactory or true conclusion could be expected; whereas, in the first syllogism, a true conclusion resulted, inasmuch as both supporting premises were objectively true, in addition to the process of inference being valid.

On the other hand, it is possible for an invalid process of thought or for an invalid argument to conclude with a true proposition. Strictly speaking, if the process of reasoning is really invalid, there is no conclusion; although for convenience sake it is customary to call the proposition which purports to be the outcome of any reasoning process, the conclusion.

For instance, if we should reason in this manner:—

All Missourians are Americans;
All St. Louisans are Americans;
All St. Louisans are Missourians.

'All St. Louisans are Missourians,' the so-called conclusion of our syllogism does not follow from the premises because 'the middle term' of the syllogism,— (Americans)—is not distributed, i.e., used in its universal extension,—at least once. The 'logical fallacy' of 'the undistributed middle' will be explained in Chapter VI.

The beginner in Logic will likewise do well to observe that in some cases an invalid argument or an invalid process of thought may apparently yield a true conclusion even when both premises are false. Consider the following example:—

Elephants are rational;
Large animals are rational;
Elephants are large animals.

In this syllogism, both premises are false; the process of reasoning is formally invalid, but the conclusion is true. From this example it can be seen that even if the conclusion is true, it does not follow that the argument or process of thought is valid. To suppose that we can safely reason from the truth of the conclusion to the validity of the argument upon which the conclusion ostensibly depends, is an error against which the beginner in Logic should be on his guard. The conclusion may be known to be true on grounds other than those alleged in the premises.

Summary.—Instances of invalid argument or of invalid processes of thought can occur when:—

1. Both premises are *true;*—
2. Both premises are *false;*—
3. One premise is *true* and one is *false;*—
4. The conclusion is *true* and one or both premises are *true* or *false.*

Instances of valid argument or of valid processes of thought can occur when:—

1. Both premises are *true;*—
2. Both premises are *false;*—
3. One premise is *true* and one premise is *false;*—
4. The conclusion is *true* and *both premises* are *true.*

Important Note.—It is only when the conditions laid down in No. 4, for valid processes of thought, are fulfilled that our conclusions will have objective logical truth as well as validity. In this case, as stated previously, the argument is called 'good' as well as 'valid.'

In a succeeding chapter, a few simple rules for determining the objective truth of the premises in any particular instance of judgment or of reasoning will be given. The observance of these rules as well as those which will assure us of the validity of our processes of thought on any occasion, will guarantee that the conclusions to our arguments will be objectively true as well as valid in form. We shall thus find the study of Logic to be more practical and satisfying, because we shall thus be more insured against sophisms and fallacies.

A REVIEW OF CHAPTER II

1. Give an exact definition of Logic.
2. What is a term?
3. How many terms can there be in a simple categorical proposition?
4. Give specific definitions of:—simple apprehension;—judgment;—of immediate and mediate inference or reasoning.
5. State the threefold aim or purpose of Logic.
6. Into what three divisions does the science of Logic broadly divide itself?
7. Explain by example, the difference between the concepts of *validity* and *truth.*

8.   When may an argument or a process of thought be called *good* as well as *valid*?

9.   Is there any ground for Durant's contention that Logic is 'the art of proving anything'?

10. Summarize all the possible instances of an *invalid* and a *valid* argument.

11. If the conclusion of an argument is *true* does it follow that the argument is *valid*?

12. In what instance alone will an argument give a *true* as well as a *valid* conclusion?

EXERCISE*

With the following examples of inference, let the student test his ability to determine which are *valid*; which are *invalid*; which are examples of a *good* argument.

1.   All birds are vertebrates;
     All fishes are vertebrates;
     All birds are fishes.

2.   No triangles are squares;
     No circles are squares;
     No circles are triangles.

3.   All Parisians are Frenchmen;
     Most Frenchmen are artistic;
     Parisians are artistic.

4.   Catholic countries are backward;
     Spain is not a Catholic country;
     Spain is not backward.

5.   A good student is not a good athlete;
     Henry is a good student;
     Henry is not a good athlete.

---

*This exercise may be deferred until the student will have acquired a knowledge of the rules and technique of the syllogism; or if not deferred, reviewed, after the syllogism has been formally explained.

6. Those who get rich quickly are dishonest;
   Smith got rich over night;
   Smith must be dishonest.

7. All circles are round;
   A baseball is round;
   A baseball is a circle.

8. All quadrilaterals are squares;
   All rectangles are squares;
   All rectangles are quadrilaterals.

9. Circles are round;
   Billiard balls are round;
   Billiard balls are circles.

10. All quadrupeds are animals;
    All horses are quadrupeds;
    All horses are animals.

11. All Spaniards are unprogressive;
    Spaniards are Catholics;
    All Catholics are unprogressive.

12. All wood is combustible;
    Some chairs are not combustible;
    Some chairs are not wood.

CHAPTER III

IDEAS OR CONCEPTS AND TERMS

The Object of Our Thought.—When we think, we have to think about something: our thought must have an object. But the object of our thought need not necessarily be something actual or material; all that is necessary is that it be not nothing. In other words, it is sufficient that the object of our thought be some kind of being or reality. It may be only a possible reality, or again, it may be an actual but immaterial reality; or it may be an actual spiritual reality; or, finally, it may be both an actual and a material reality.

It is of the greatest importance for clear, logical thought that we be able to determine in any and in every instance of thinking, just what kind of reality is represented in our minds by our concepts or ideas.

Reality is not always of the same kind then, whenever it is represented to our minds. It is represented to us by means of our ideas or concepts in quite a number of distinct variations.

Terms.—Terms, in general, are the oral or written expression of the objects of our ideas, just as they are represented to the mind.*

---

*According to St. Thomas terms stand for the objects of our ideas: they are not the expression of the subjective concept as such nor of things as they are in nature. They stand for things precisely as the mind conceives them. "Voces referuntur ad res significandas mediante conceptione intellectus." (Sum. Theol. I q. 13 a. 1.)

Whenever we write or utter a term, we announce in effect, that some particular reality is represented in our minds. Very often the representation of the reality in our minds is hazy or not clear, and then we err in giving it expression: either we use the incorrect term, or, although using the correct term, we intend it to stand for more content of representation in the mind than is warranted.

"The beginning of genuine culture," Socrates is reported to have said, "is the scrutiny of general terms."— Epictetus, Dissert. 1, 17.

Purpose of Chapter Three.—The purpose of Chapter Three is to give briefly, a few notions on the varieties of reality which can be represented in our minds as the object of our ideas or concepts; and secondly, to explain the nature of the various kinds of ideas and of the terms which we are constantly making use of to give expression to the object of our ideas. Ability to discriminate terms; a facility in recognizing the limits of the representation in the mind according to the measurement of any term in any particular instance, is essential for the student of Logic; it is a fundamental sine-qua-non for clear and exact thinking.

The Different Kinds of Being or Reality.—Anything is a 'being' or a 'reality' which is not nothing. Anything is not nothing whose concept does not involve a contradiction as would the concept of a 'square circle' or 'a finite God.'

Possible Being or Possible Reality.—In the first place, the notion of being or reality applies to possible being or reality. A possible being or reality is one which although it does not exist in the actual order of things, nevertheless, it is capable of so existing, inasmuch as its concept or its representation in the mind involves no contradiction. A possible being is a reality but in the order of possibilities, not actualities. As such, it is something, it is not nothing, and it may be an object of an idea, i.e., something about which it is possible to think. God cannot be a possible being.

Immaterial Being.—An immaterial being or reality is any inextended being or reality. More commonly we seem to think of immaterial beings or realities as actually existing although the definition includes immaterial beings or realities in the order of possibles, e.g., possible justice or possible charity. Justice, patriotism, charity themselves, are actual immaterial things.

Spiritual Beings or Spiritual Realities.—Spiritual beings or realities are inextended immaterial realities, which of themselves, independently, are capable of action, e.g., God, an angel, the human soul. A being which is simply immaterial does not connote the independent power of action. Finite spiritual beings like simple immaterial beings, may be in the order of possibles.

Material Beings or Realities.—A material being or reality is an extended reality. A material reality may also exist in the order of possibles, e.g., 'a possible world different from our own.' Although we can perceive most material beings with our senses, there are some which we cannot so perceive, e.g., gravity, electricity, an atom, an ion, the soul of a brute.

Classification of Ideas.—Ideas may be considered from the standpoint of quality and from the standpoint of quantity, i.e., we may consider in what way the idea represents its object to the mind, and then, secondly, the number of objects which may be included in the extension of the object as represented in the mind.*

CLASSIFICATION OF IDEAS FROM THE STANDPOINT OF QUALITY

Concrete Ideas.—Perhaps the most common kind of an idea is a concrete idea. A concrete idea is one which represents its object just as it is in nature, i.e., as a quality or as a number of qualities together with the subject in which the quality or qualities inhere, e.g., this red house, this little boy, George Washington. A concrete term is any oral or written expression which stands for the object of a concrete idea.**

Abstract Ideas.—An abstract idea is one which represents its object as a quality separated from or abstracted from its subject or the subject as separated, abstracted from its qualities. Think of the 'white' of this paper, for instance, represented to the mind as separated from or abstracted from the paper. It is thus represented to the mind in an abstract manner, as 'whiteness.' 'Whiteness' is an abstract term. An abstract term, then, is one which stands for the object of an abstract

---

* See definition of 'Extension of Terms', p. 35.

**A word which by itself is capable of standing for the object of an idea is called a 'categorematic term.' Such words which are capable of standing for the object of an idea, only in composition with other words, are called 'syncategorematic terms.' Conjunctions, prepositions, adverbs, e.g., are of this class of terms.

idea, i.e., for something represented to the mind as separated from, or abstracted from the concrete object as it is in nature.

Clear, Distinct, Obscure, Confused Ideas.—An idea is a clear idea when it represents its object to the mind in such a way that we can distinguish that object from other objects. The opposite of a clear, is an obscure idea, i.e., one which does not give sufficient number of the characteristics of the object of the idea to distinguish it from other objects. An idea is a distinct idea when its object is represented to the mind in such a way that we can indicate the points of difference between it and other objects in addition to being able to distinguish it from other objects. The opposite of a distinct idea is a confused idea. For instance, the person who has only a confused idea of St. Peter's in Rome would be unable to tell just how it differs in detail, from The Cathedral of Cologne.

Positive Ideas.—A positive idea is one which represents a thing by means of attributes that it really possesses, e.g., life, light.

THE UNIVOCAL, EQUIVOCAL AND THE ANALOGOUS USE OF TERMS

A term is used **univocally** when it is repeatedly used in the same sense or meaning in any designated instance of oral or written speech.

The designated instance of speech may be only a sentence or a paragraph or it may be a long essay, an oration, a book or a volume.

A term is used **equivocally** when in any designated instance of speech, it is used repeatedly, but each time with an altogether different meaning, although each time the term is used, it is either written or pronounced in the same way.

It should be noted that when a term is used equivocally, there is no relationship between the different objects for which the term stands.

The **analogous** use of a term is somewhat more complicated. To begin with, when a term is said to be used analogously, it is not used in the fullest content of meaning which the term has or is capable of having. As a consequence, a term used analogously, never stands for the complete or the exact objective truth.

A term is used analogously when as an adjective modifier it is applied to an object which in itself is incapable of having the quality or property thus attributed to it by the adjective modifier, but which nevertheless, has some extrinsic relationship with that object to which the term in question or the adjective modifier can be applied with the full content of its meaning.

For instance, we apply the term "healthy" to climate and the color of one's skin. Now nothing but a living organism can be healthy in the full sense of the word. But climate and the color of one's skin have an extrinsic relationship to living organisms, the former as a cause of health; the latter as a sign of it. The term "healthy," therefore, is applied to climate and to the color of one's skin not in the full sense of the word, but in an improper, analogous way.

Secondly, a term is used analogously, when as the predicate of a proposition it indicates that the subject of

DOMINICAN COLLEGE
LIBRARY
SAN RAFAEL

the proposition is predicated as having in a limited way the same kind or a similar kind of reality which some other subject or subjects have in the fullest sense.

For instance, to predicate of any person or thing the attribute of "being" is to use the term "being" analogously. When we predicate "being" of anything except God, we are predicating it in the limited sense of dependent being. Of God alone can "being" be predicated in the fullest sense of the term, because of God alone is it the essence or the nature to be, simply or absolutely.

All metaphorical predicate terms or words are in effect, analogous predications in the sense just explained.

Finally, a term is used analogously, when it denotes some action upon an object which is not the proper object to receive the act signified. A term is used analogously in this instance, because the action now indicated by it on an improper object has the relationship of similarity to the same action on its proper object. Example: the ships are ploughing the deep.

Contrariwise, a term is used analogously when it indicates a subject incapable of being truly acted upon in the way it is signified as acted upon, but nevertheless, thus acted upon, the result is similar to that which occurs when the proper subject for the art signified, is acted upon. Example: The ploughed-up waters of the ocean dash against rocks.

CLASSIFICATION OF IDEAS AND TERMS FROM THE STANDPOINT OF QUANTITY

Universal Ideas.—An universal idea is one which represents its object to the mind as something which is common to many objects; or, to be precise, as something which is common to all the individuals in a particular class of objects. The attribute which happens to be the object of a universal idea is predicable of the whole class and of each individual member of the class. I can equally predicate 'man,' for instance, of 'all men' and of Peter, James, John, etc., individually.

Extension of Terms.—The extension of a term means the number of individuals in any particular class of things to which the term is applicable.

Sometimes we use a term to stand for the object of our idea in all of its extension and then our term is said to be an 'universal term,' e.g., all men. Sometimes we use a term to stand for the object of our idea in only part of its extension or indefinitely, and then our term is said to be a 'particular term,' e.g., some men.

Comprehension of Terms.—The comprehension of a term means the attributes, qualities or characteristics which the term implies and which must be present in the object of an idea before the term can be applied to it. The term 'negro' for instance, means a man of black color. This means I am using the term 'negro' for those attributes which must be present in the object represented by the term; first, the general attributes of a man (body with life, sensation, reason), and second, the special attribute of a negro,—black color.

Collective Terms.—A collective term is one which stands for the object of an idea as a reality which includes all the individuals of a particular class of things taken as a unit, e.g., the army, the navy.

Singular Terms.—A singular term is one which expresses the object of an idea represented to the mind as a definite, individual thing, e.g., this house, Abraham Lincoln, St. Peter's Cathedral in Rome.

For purposes of Logic, singular terms are equivalent to universal terms, since they express the object as equivalent to a definite class of thing, in which class there is only one member or individual,—the object itself in question.

Supposition of Terms.—The supposition of a term is the definite meaning which a term has in a given context. A term is said to have a material supposition when the object of the idea which it represents is the term itself. Thus when the term, 'Peter', is taken to mean a word of two syllables, the term, 'Peter', is used in a material supposition. A term is used in logical supposition when it stands for the object of a concept taken in the abstract,—as a class of things or as a species, e.g., 'man', when it stands for the species, 'man'. A term is said to have real supposition when it is used as standing for one or more of the individuals of any particular class of things as they actually exist in nature, e.g., this red house, these few boys.

Quantifying Adjectives.—It is easy enough to tell that the subject term of a proposition is intended to be taken as an universal term when the term is modified by those quantitative adjectives which signify all the objects in any particular class of things. Such quantifying adjectives are: **all, every, any, whichever, whatever;** and the negatives: **no, none, and, not any.** It is likewise easy to recognize the subject term of a proposition as particular in extension or quantity, when it is modified by such adjectives which denote less than the total number of the subjects in any designated class of things. When there is no quantitative adjective modifying a given subject term of a proposition, the term as a general rule, is intended to be universal in form or extension. Instinct for, or familiarity with one's own language will almost always be a safe guide in helping us to determine whether a non-quantified subject term registers on us as 'universal' or 'particular' in form, or extension. To determine whether a subject term of a proposition which does register on us as 'universal in form,' has any warrant to be considered truly universal from the standpoint of objective truth, is another question. In a following chapter, a few simple rules will be given to enable us to determine when such subject terms, 'universal in form,' are to be considered 'universal in fact.'

Whether a term in the predicate position is 'universal' or 'particular' in quantity or extension depends on the affirmative or negative character of the proposition. The rules for determining the quantity of the predicate will be given in the following chapter.*

---

*By itself, an adjective term has *no extension* unless it is used in place of a noun. Prepositions, adverbs, or conjunctions cannot be called terms.

Only verbs in the infinitive mood or in the form of the gerund participle can be considered as terms.

In fine, only such words or such combination of words which are capable of standing for an idea, or the object of an idea, are terms.

QUESTIONS FOR REVIEW

1. Name the different kinds of reality about which we can think.
2. Explain the nature of these different kinds of reality.
3. Define a concrete idea; an abstract idea.
4. Explain the difference between a clear and an obscure idea. Explain the difference between a distinct and a confused idea.
5. What is a positive idea? What is a negative idea?
6. When is a term said to be univocal? equivocal? analogous?
7. Explain how metaphorical terms are terms used analogously.
8. Define an universal idea.
9. What is meant by the extension of a term?
10. When are terms said to be universal? When particular? When singular?
11. Why are singular terms treated as universal terms in Logic?
12. What is a collective term?
13. What is meant by the supposition of a term?
14. Explain what is meant by the material, the logical and the real supposition of a term.
15. Enumerate the quantifying adjectives which indicate that a term in the subject position of a proposition is particular in form or extension.
16. When there is no quantifying adjective modifying a term in the subject position of a proposition, what is the form or extension of this term?

EXERCISE

What kind of being or reality is represented to the mind by the *italicized* single terms, or by the *italicized* compound terms in the following propositions and statements?

1. *God* is a *spirit*.
2. *Patriotism* is a *virtue* which inclines one to love his country.

3. *The Chicago World's Fair of 1933* was held in *Grant Park*.
4. *The end of the world* is *something* no man can predict.
5. Poor *Fido* is dead! What has become of his *soul?*
6. *Electricity* is perhaps the *busiest servant in the world.*
7. *"He* hath given His *angels* charge over *thee."*
8. *Honesty* is the best *policy.*
9. *Man* is a synonym for *humanity.*
10. *Nature* and *Nature's God* are two distinctly different objects.
11. Picture to yourself *a hundred-headed elephant.*
12. A *point* has neither length, breadth or thickness. What kind of a reality is it?

In the following propositions or statements: State which single or compound *italicized* terms are concrete; which abstract; which in the subject position are universal; which particular; which singular.

1. *These students* are *diligent.*
2. *A student of Logic* is one who is learning how to think.
3. *Paul* is standing among *those athletes over there.*
4. *An athlete* may be *a student.*
5. *Not all these lawyers* are making *a living.*
6. There is a speck of *dirt* on *your white Arrow collar.*
7. *Justice* is a virtue which inclines us to give to another his due.
8. Many *(?)* admire virtue: few *(?)* practice it.*
9. *Some of the students in this course* are in *danger* of failure.
10. *These young children* of today are the *men* and *women* of tomorrow.

---

* When a noun which the adjective term modifies is not expressed but understood, it is called an *eliptical term.* An *eliptical term* must be expressed, not left understood, in order to answer correctly the questions which are asked in this exercise. Notice how many of the *eliptical terms* in the sentences above are indicated by *question marks.*

An *elipsis* also occurs when in a compound proposition of two subjects having the same predicate, the predicate is expressed with the first subject, but is understood with the second.

In the following propositions and statements, state: Which single or compound *italicized* terms are used univocally; which equivocally; which analogously.

1. Look at the farmers *ploughing* the field; see the ships *ploughing* the deep.
2. John has a *taste* for olives but not *(?)* for literateure.
3. Both minerals and organisms are *corporeal substances*.
4. *To lie* is restful but according to Ethics *to lie* is evil.
5. A man is *an animal* but so too is a horse *(?)*
6. An angel is *a spiritual being* but so too is a man a *(?)*
7. The road over Mt. Athos is *rough* but not as *rough* as the road to success.
8. People are generally *healthy* in a *healthy* climate.
9. There are too many *bulls* in the world; Irish *bulls*; Papal *bulls*; *bulls* in the stock market; *bulls* on the cattle ranges.
10. He is a *bear* for punishment.

State the supposition of each italicized term in the following propositions and statements:

1. *Cicero* is a word of three syllables: *Cicero* was an orator.
2. *Zev* won the derby. *Zev* was a famous *horse*. *Horse* is a class of animals. Zev therefore is a whole class of animals and a whole class of animals won the derby.
3. This Ford is not an *automobile* because an *automobile* is a word of four syllables.
4. What is the difference between *God* and *The Divinity?*
5. This *man* is Paul: *man* means humanity: therefore, Paul is humanity.

CHAPTER IV

JUDGMENTS AND PROPOSITIONS

Judgment.—Whenever we make an affirmative or negative statement, we are expressing a judgment. A judgment is an act of the mind by which we affirm or deny the identity between the objects of two ideas.

We must note well that when we affirm or deny by means of a proposition as the expression of a judgment, what we affirm or deny is not an identity between two ideas but an identity between the objects of two ideas, e.g., the judgment: 'A rose is a plant,' does not mean: —'the idea rose' is 'the idea plant.' It means that a 'real rose'—possible or actual—is a 'real plant'—possible or actual. The judgment: 'No square is a circle' does not mean:—'the idea square' is not 'the idea circle,'— but that in the real order of things outside the mind, whether in the possible or actual order,—no square is a circle.

Categorical Propositions.—Categorical propositions are those in which the predicate is affirmed or denied of the subject, simply, e.g., Man is a rational animal.

Validity or Consistency of Judgments.—Our judgments are valid and consistent, if there is no contradiction expressed or implied in them. This does not mean that a valid or consistent judgment necessarily represents objective logical truth, e.g., 'Some of the students in this class are lazy', is a judgment which implies no contradiction, but it may not be a judgment which represents real objective logical truth.

Logical Form.—It is imperative for a beginner to learn how to express all categorical statements in logical form. A categorical statement is expressed in logical form when and only when it is expressed by means of the logical copula, (is, am, or are). A statement expressed by means of the logical copula is not only a statement but a proposition as well. The copula (is, am, or are) is the only verb Logic recognizes when dealing with categorical and disjunctive propositions.

Conditional statements are not restricted for expression to the logical copula. Even when conditional statements are not expressed by means of the logical copula, it is customary to call such statements, conditional propositions.

Logical Subject and Logical Predicate.*—Logic does not agree with grammar in its notion of subject and predicate. Grammatically, we may have a group of words preceding the principal verb of any simple categorical statement, or the copula of any simple categorical proposition, of which group, only the principal noun or pronoun is the grammatical subject of the sentence or of the proposition. Similarly, of a group of words following the copula of a proposition, only

---

* The importance of understanding the difference between the 'grammatical subject' and the 'logical subject'; between the grammatical predicate and the logical predicate, will be appreciated especially, when it is necessary to analyze a major or a minor premise of a syllogism for the exact 'middle term,' or for the unwarranted presence of four terms in a syllogism.

the principal noun or pronoun of the group is the grammatical predicate. But the 'logical subject' of any statement or proposition consists of the group of words itself which precede the principal verb of a statement or proposition, taken as a unit: the 'logical predicate,' likewise, is a group of words taken as a unit which in a proposition follow the copula. (See p. 58 for examples of statements recast into logical form.)*

THE READING OR ANALYSIS OF CATEGORICAL PROPOSITIONS

A categorical proposition is one which affirms or denies an attribute—(the predicate)—of the subject of a proposition, simply or without any qualification.

A simple categorical proposition is one which affirms or denies simply, one and only one attribute of the subject of a proposition. In a simple categorical proposition not only must the predicate be numerically one but the subject must be one without numerical restriction. This means the subject must not be limited by such words as "except," "but" or "save." Nor should the word "only" be found in the subject term, for its presence in the subject term implies that the subject is restricted by the term, "and no others."

John is a student. This is a simple categorical proposition. But consider the following propositions: All the boys except John are athletes. This is a categorical proposition whose subject "all the boys" is numerically restricted by the subtraction of one boy, John, as the term "except" indicates.

In this proposition: Only John is present at the lecture,—the term "only" implies that the subject, John, is restricted by the implied term,—"and no others."

Similarly, the words "but" and "save" imply numerical restriction of a subject if they modify it in the sense of "except," e.g., All the boys but James are studious. All the students save a few are certain to pass.

Such propositions, then, are not simple but complex categorical propositions. They are, like grammatically compound propositions, exponable. More about exponable propositions farther on.

It should be noted that a grammatically complex proposition which has the subject of its principal clause modified by a relative or a temporal clause, is not exponable, and hence in Logic is regarded as a simple categorical proposition, e.g., Any student who studies intelligently is worthy of praise. The time when we are discouraged is the time when we ought to be most cheerful.

No categorical proposition can be logically analyzed with satisfaction, until it is cast or recast into the form of a simple categorical proposition. To read or analyze a proposition logically, therefore, the first thing to do is to see that it is cast in the form of a simple categorical proposition.

Reading or analyzing simple categorical propositions means analyzing them for their quantity and their quality. The quantity of a simple categorical proposition means its universal or particular character: the quality of a simple categorical proposition means its affirmative or negative character.

When we speak of the quantity of terms or propositions, both terms and propositions are either universal or particular. When we speak of the quality of propositions we refer to their affirmative or negative character.

When we speak of the quality of terms or ideas, however, they are never affirmative or negative, but, above all, concrete, or abstract, for purposes of logical analysis.

HOW TO TELL THE QUANTITY OF A PROPOSITION

The quantity of a proposition is the same as the quantity of its subject term. If the subject term is universal in extension or quantity, the proposition is said to be universal; if the subject term is particular in quantity, the proposition is particular in quantity. Disregard the predicate term when reading a proposition for quantity.

Two Kinds of Quantity.—It should be noted that Logic, ignoring the more definite numerical designations, reduces all quantity to two kinds, universal and particular. As explained before, singular propositions are treated in Logic as universals. Reading every proposition either as a universal or a particular is known as the extensive or the inclusive mode of reading them. It is the method adhered to in this book.

Universal Affirmative or 'A' Propositions.—The presence of such quantifying adjectives as:— all, every, any, whatever, and the like, as well as the adjective pronoun, anyone, in the logical subject term of a proposition, tells us at once that the subject term itself and hence the proposition is universal in quantity. Universal affirmative propositions are designated in Logic by the capital letter, 'A.'

Universal Negative, or 'E' Propositions.—Whenever it is considered necessary to express the quantifying adjective in a universal negative proposition, the proposition should not be expressed in the form: 'All are not etc.', or, 'Everyone is not, etc.' To be specific, such quantifying adjectives should not introduce the proposition, nor should the negative 'not' follow the copula in these instances of universal negative propositions. For example, do not write: 'All men are not angels.' Such a form for a negative universal is ambiguous. By stressing the quantifying adjective in the example just given, it is made to register not as a universal, but as a particular negative proposition.

The correct way to express an universal negative proposition when the quantifying adjective is expressed, is to introduce the proposition with the negative universal adjectives: 'no', 'none' or 'not any', and then, to omit the negative 'not' after the copula, e.g., 'No man is an angel.'

When the quantifying adjective is not expressed but implied in an universal negative proposition, the proposition may be written correctly and without ambiguity, in the form in which the negative 'not' follows the copula, e.g., 'Men are not angels;' or, 'Wealth is not an attraction to some men.'

Some Peculiar Propositions. — Some propositions may seem to the unwary to be negative when in reality, they are strictly affirmative. For example, in the following proposition:—Not to complain in adversity is a mark of a great soul,—the negative 'not' simply negates 'to complain';—it does not affect the copula. In every instance where the word 'not' introduces a proposition having for its subject term an 'infinitive' or an 'infinitive phrase', and provided there is no second negative modifying the copula, the proposition is affirmative not negative.*

For a proposition to be negative, the negative 'not' must affect the copula. Now, in particular, this is always the case with propositions introduced by the words, 'not all' and hence all propositions introduced by 'not all' are negative as well as particular, e.g., Not all that glitters is gold.†

Particular Propositions.—Whenever the subject term of a proposition contains the quantifying adjectives: 'some', 'few', 'most', 'hardly any', or any other quantifying adjective equivalent to these, the subject and hence the proposition, is particular in quantity. If particular propositions are affirmative, they are designated in Logic by the capital letter 'I'; if negative, by the capital letter 'O'.

Non-Quantified Propositions.—When a proposition contains no quantifying adjective word among those which make up the subject term of the proposition, to indicate the quantity of the proposition explicitly, the proposition registers on us as a universal in form, e.g., Children are noisy;—Women are jealous. Whether such

---

* Propositions beginning with an 'infinitive' or an 'infinitive phrase' are always universal in form.

† 'Not all that glitters is gold.'—This proposition may also be written in strict Logical form:—Some things which glitter are not gold. It may follow, indeed, that:—Some things which glitter are gold,—but that is not what is *explicitly* stated when we write, either:—Not all that glitters is gold, or, Some things which glitter are not gold.

The student in Logic must learn to restrict himself to just what is stated or to the exact proposition as it is proposed to him or written before him. In regard to this particular proposition just stated and with others like it, it has been the experience of the writer, that it takes time to convince some students that the proposition is not the same as the inferred proposition: Some things which glitter are gold.

propositions have any warrant to be considered universal propositions from the standpoint of objective truth is another question.

And this is an important question, for the reason that the fertile source of innumerable errors, fallacies and sophisms in the oral and written speech of men can be traced to this very thing;—that propositions which register as universal in form are taken to be universal likewise from the standpoint of objective truth.

The following rule will serve as a norm for determining the objective truth of both quantified and non-quantified propositions which register as universal in form.

An Important Rule.—No proposition, whether explicity quantified as a universal in form or whether it is a non-quantified proposition registering as an universal in form, has any warrant to be considered an universal proposition from the standpoint of objective truth, unless it is, either:

(1)   A proposition expressing an 'a priori' judgment;

(2)   A proposition stating a physical or scientific law;

(3)   A proposition stating the nature or a property of a human being.*†

The following excerpt lends a forcible point to the content of the 'important rule' just stated.

"Sound logic is not always desirable. It is in fact, the most dangerous of all things if one starts with *false* premises. In such

---

* In the case of singular propositions, which are historical, if they are not obviously true we can know them to be such, if the witnesses of them are found to have an actual knowledge of what the proposition states, and at the same time these witnesses are proven to be men of veracity.

†See definition of a property on page 132.

a case the more logically one reasons, the further one gets from the truth. The only hope there is for a healthy conclusion or a good thought, if the premise is false, is to make a terrible slip somewhere in the reasoning process. "Crooked roads sometimes get us back on the right road if we have lost our way, but if the wrong road is a straight road we are lost forever."—Fulton Sheen, *Old Errors and New Labels,* p. 287.

Again in regard to the point just treated in the 'important rule' it might be advantageous also when studying or teaching Logic to reflect on the following excerpt:

"Logicians are more set upon concluding rightly than on right conclusions. They cannot see the end for the process."—Newman's *Grammar of Assent,* p. 94.

'A Priori' Propositions.—An 'a priori' proposition is one which has for its predicate a term expressing some attribute of the subject which is necessarily implied in the subject in such a way, that a full understanding of the subject and the predicate is sufficient without any experiment on a particular case, to make us see that the truth of the proposition holds in all cases; absolutely, and without any possible exception, e.g., Circles are round.

'A Posteriori' Propositions.—An 'a posteriori' proposition is one which expresses a judgment based on experience, e.g., Metals are conductors of electricity.

According to the 'important rule,' just given, it follows that an 'a posteriori' proposition expressed as an universal in form,—stands for real objective truth, if the proposition states a physical or scientific law; or, if it gives expression to a judgment which is in accordance with the nature of a human being. Students of Logic at times seem to imagine that a proposition which is both universal in form and at the same time gives objective truth, must necessarily be an 'a priori' proposition. All 'a priori' propositions are, to be sure, universal in form and in fact, i.e., give objective truth,—but not all universals in form which express objective truth, are 'a priori' propositions.

The Quantity of the Predicate.—The predicate of an affirmative proposition is always particular in quantity, the predicate of a negative proposition is always universal in quantity.*

It follows that since the predicate of an affirmative proposition is particular in quantity; in every affirmative proposition, the predicate is always implicitly modified by the word 'some.' For example, Men are mortal. This means: Men are *some* of the mortal things in the world. Some roses are red. This means: Some roses are *some* of the real, possible or actual red things in the world. On the other hand, we must be careful to understand the analysis of the predicate of a negative proposition. It is always universal in quantity or as it is expressed in Logic, it is always 'distributed'. For example, No man is an angel. This means: No man is to be numbered among *any* of the angels, possible or actual. —Some roses are not red. This means: Some roses are *not any* of the things—possible or actual—ever to be numbered among *any* 'red' things.

---

* The predicate of an affirmative proposition, is *universal in quantity or extension* whenever the predicate states *the essential definition of the subject* and whenever the predicate term of a proposition stands for the identical object represented by the subject term, e.g., Paul is the third boy on the left.

Exponable propositions are those non-simple categorical propositions which must be resolved or divided into two or more propositions in order to bring out their true meaning. It is impossible to deal with exponables for purposes of Logic until they are broken up into the simple propositions of which they are composed. Exponables are of two kinds. First, all grammatically compound propositions are exponables, e.g., Milwaukee is a large and beautiful city; or, Milwaukee and Chicago are neighboring cities. The first of these propositions, for purposes of Logic becomes: Milwaukee is a large city,—Milwaukee is a beautiful city; the second: Milwaukee is a neighboring city to Chicago,—Chicago is a neighboring city to Milwaukee.

The second class of exponables consists of those propositions which are modified by some limitative or restrictive word, such as: 'except,' 'but,' 'alone,' 'save,' and the like. For example, All the boys in the Latin class except John are studious. This means Peter, James, Bill, Tom, etc., are studious,—John is not studious. Notice how exponables of this second class resolve into one affirmative and one negative proposition. Such exponables are 'complex categorical' as explained before. (See p. 44.)*

A grammatical complex proposition, i.e., one whose subject is modified by a relative or temporal clause; in Logic, is a simple categorical, (See p. 44), e.g., The stu-

---

* In breaking up exponables of this kind into the simple categorical propositions of which they are composed, always express the simple negative proposition first. For example: All the students in the class except John are studious: should be expressed as two simple categoricals in this way: John is not studious; All the other students in the class are studious.

dents who have studied, are those who will pass;—The hour at which you are due, is four o'clock. Similarly the proposition in which the subject is modified by an adverbial clause must be considered as equivalent, in Logic, to a simple categorical proposition, e.g., The house where I was born, is now the little red school house of the town.

NON-CATEGORICAL PROPOSITIONS

In this chapter, thus far, we have treated of categorical propositions only,—those which affirm or deny simply. There are two other varieties, known to Logic, —conditional and disjunctive propositions.

A conditional proposition is one which neither asserts nor denies simply, like a categorical proposition, but it is one which makes an assertion or denial, dependently on the truth or, at least, the consistency of another proposition, e.g., If Caesar was ambitious, he deserved to die. There is no practical value to the question of whether conditional propositions have quantity and quality.

A disjunctive proposition is one which offers two or more alternatives, i.e., two or more alternative assertions or denials, e.g., Either he is honest, or he is dishonest. Disjunctive propositions are always affirmative in quality. The negation of alternatives would not result in a disjunctive but in so many negative categorical propositions; e.g., Man is neither a plant nor a mineral, is equal to: Man is not a plant, and man is not a mineral.

Logic of Conditional Propositions.—For one thing, when we are dealing with conditional propositions, we

must disregard the rules peculiar to categorical propositions. The logic of conditional propositions is not based
on the laws of quantity, quality, etc., as is the case with
categoricals. All that we have to remember about conditional propositions are these two points:

(1) The one part of a conditional proposition,—the
part expressed with 'if' or the dependent clause of the
proposition, is called the antecedent; the other part is
called the consequent; (2) Conditional propositions are
valid in an argument or in any process of thought, only
when there is a necessary connection between the antecedent and the consequent, or in other words, only
when the consequent necessarily follows from the antecedent.*

The Nature of Disjunctive Propositions.—In regard
to disjunctive propositions, they are valid, and at the
same time they are trustworthy expressions of objective logical truth when: (1) The alternatives expressed
are mutually exclusive; (2) all the alternatives are expressed. The following examples violate one or the
other of these rules: Either he is a fool or a knave.—
(He might be both.)—All men in America are either
white, brown or red.—(What about negroes?)

---

* The necessary connection between the antecedent and the consequent need not be a *metaphysical* one, i.e., one to which there could be
no exception even by the power of God. It is sufficient that the necessary
connection be either a *physical* or a *moral* necessity, i.e., one either according to the physical laws of Nature, or one according to the nature of
human being.

QUESTIONS FOR REVIEW

1. When we make a judgment do we affirm or deny an identity between two ideas or between the two objects of the ideas?

2. When are our judgments *valid* or *consistent?*

3. Explain the difference between: (a) The logical subject and the grammatical subject of a proposition: (b) Between the logical predicate and the grammatical predicate.

4. What is meant by *the quantity of a proposition?* By the *quality?*

5. What is the general rule for reading the quantity of a simple categorical proposition?

6. How many kinds of quantity does Logic recognize?

7. How are universal affirmative propositions designated in Logic? universal negatives? particular affirmatives? particular negatives?

8. What is the correct form in which to write or state a universal negative proposition when there is a quantifying adjective in the logical subject?

9. Explain how some peculiar universal propositions which seem to be negative are really affirmative.

10. What is to be noted about propositions introduced by the words: 'not all'?

11. How do non-quantified propositions register on us as to form?

12. What is the important rule for determining the *objective truth* of a proposition which registers as a *universal in form?*

13. Define an 'a priori' proposition.

14. Define an 'a posteriori' proposition.

15. Is it possible for 'a posteriori' propositions to be *universally true* as well as to be *universal in form?*

16. How is the quantity of the predicate of a proposition determined?
17. What are exponable propositions?
18. Demonstrate by examples how the two varieties of exponables should be treated for purposes of Logic.
19. Define a conditional proposition. Define a disjunctive proposition.
20. State the Logic of both conditional and disjunctive propositions.

EXERCISES

In the following examples: (a) Express all statements in logical form. (b) Point out the grammatical and logical subjects and predicates. (c) Tell the quantity and quality of the propositions. (d) If any of the propositions are universal according to form, determine whether they have any warrant to be so considered from the standpoint of *truth*. (e) Which propositions are exponable? (f) Which propositions are 'a priori'? Which are 'a posteriori'?

1. Birds sing.
2. Man reasons.
3. John won the race.
4. Mary studied her lesson.
5. Honest men deserve praise.
6. No good deeds go unrewarded.
7. Full many a flower is born to blush unseen.
8. What prevented me from recognizing you was your new hat.
9. It is better to fight for the good than to rail at the wicked.
10. Wealth attracts men.
11. All trees are plants.

12. Circles are round.
13. Fire burns.
14. No man is an angel.
15. No wise man runs into danger needlessly.
16. No good deeds are useless.
17. Many habits are hurtful.
18. Not every crime is detected.
19. A triangle is a plane figure bounded by three straight lines.
20. He that makes haste to be rich is not innocent.
21. Everything that is wise has been thought already.
22. The patient who makes the doctor his heir, is not likely to recover.
23. No person who is not a great sculptor or painter, can be an architect.
24. Whatever is not metallic, is not capable of magnetic influence.
25. Some substances which do not possess gravity are immaterial.
26. All are not wise who read much.
27. A noisy man is ever in the right.
28. All lawyers are not formalists.
29. Sorry her lot who loves too well.
30. Not all who are called are chosen.
31. What can't be cured must be endured.
32. Few candidates were satisfactory.
33. Whatever is, is right.
34. All that glitters is not gold.
35. Not to complain is a sign of a great soul.
36. Haste makes waste.
37. Asbestos is a non-inflammable substance.
38. Only material bodies gravitate.

39. Only the wise are prudent.
40. Anyone but an idiot would believe it.
41. The man I don't like is the man I don't know.
42. All except John passed the examination.

*   *   *   *

In which of the following conditional propositions is there a necessary connection between antecedent and consequent?

1. If he is an American citizen in good standing, he has a right to vote.
2. If a country is well governed, the people are happy.
3. If he is a good player, he will make the team.
4. If he is industrious, he will succeed.
5. If there is a God, He is a just God.
6. If God is infinite, He has all perfection.
7. If Caesar was ambitious, he deserved to die.
8. If it gets colder tonight, the lake will freeze.
9. If all men were just, there would be no need of valor.
10. If a man is educated, he does not want to work with his hands.

*   *   *   *

Which of the following disjunctive propositions are valid?

1. He is either a Frenchman, an Italian or a Spaniard.
2. Either there is a future life, or wickedness remains unpunished.
3. Every blood vessel is either a vein or an artery.
4. He is either a student or an athlete.
5. He is either very timid or very modest.
6. John did not pass either because he used poor text books or because he was badly taught.
7. Either the witness is perjured, or the prisoner is guilty.
8. He is either just fifty, or under fifty, or past fifty.

VARIETIES OF SPEECH RECAST IN LOGICAL FORM

1. A horse! A horse! My kingdom for a horse! (Expon.)
   A horse is what I ardently desire. (I)
   My kingdom is the price I would pay for a horse. (A)

2. He who never felt a wound is he who jests at scars.
   Those who never suffered from a wound are accustomed to jest at scars. (A)

3. Long live the king!
   That the king may live long is what I sincerely wish. (A) or (I)

4. I die by the help of too many physicians. (Alexander the Great)
   The cause of my death is help given to me by too many physicians. (A)

5. All flowers are not for nosegays. (Ambiguous)
   Not all flowers are for nosegays. (O) or
   Some flowers are not for nosegays. (O)

6. Send a fool to the market and a fool he'll return.
   A fool sent to the market is a fool returning from the market. (A)

7. In the resurrection they shall neither marry nor be married but shall be as the Angels of God in heaven.—Matt. xxii., 30. (Exponable)
   Marriage is a thing which will be unknown after the resurrection. (A)
   Men are beings, destined after the resurrection, to be even as the Angels of God in heaven. (A)

8. None but the brave deserve the fair. (Exponable)
   No coward is worthy of the fair. (E)
   The brave are those who deserve the fair. (A)

9. Believe if thou wilt that mountains change their places, but believe not that men change their dispositions. (Mahomet). (Exponable)
   That mountains should change their places is believable. (A)
   That men change their dispositions is unbelievable. (A)

10. No question is settled until it is settled right.
    No wrongly settled question is a settled question. (E)
11. They who never think always talk.
    They who never think are those who always talk. (A)

Note how these examples bring out the fact that a term is not necessarily one word. A term is one word or any group of words expressing an idea.

CHAPTER V

IMMEDIATE INFERENCE

It was the purpose of the preceding chapter to analyze the nature of the act of judgment in itself and to explain the rules which we must observe in forming our judgments if we wish to form them consistently or without contradicting ourselves. The present chapter has for its purpose both to acquaint us with the several ways we may logically proceed to infer immediately, a new judgment or proposition from any given judgment or proposition; and secondly, to explain the rules we must observe to make valid inferences according to these several modes of immediate inference.

Immediate inference, it will be remembered from Chapter Two,—is that act or operation of the mind by which we bring out explicitly, in a second proposition a new judgment which was implicitly contained in a given proposition, e.g., No circles are square; therefore, no squares are circles.

An act of immediate inference may proceed according to any of these several methods: opposition; conversion; obversion; contraposition, or finally, according to the method of added determinants.

Opposition.—Opposition is that species of immediate inference by which from one given proposition, we infer another having the same subject and predicate, but which differs from the given proposition either in quantity or quality or in both.

It must be remembered that two propositions which deal with different subject matter, cannot be said to have any relationship with one another. In every instance of immediate inference, the subject and predicate of the inferred proposition must have some relationship to the subject and predicate of the proposition from which the second proposition has been inferred.

From the definition of 'opposition,' it will be noted that the process of immediate inference according to the method of 'opposition,' is based on the relationships of quantity and quality between any two propositions.

There can be four and only four possible relationships between propositions based on quantity and quality. These relationships are: The relationship of contraries; contradictories; subalterns; and sub-contraries.

Contraries.—Two propositions are said to be contraries, when both,—having the same subject and the same predicate,—are universal in quantity, but differ in quality, e.g., All men are rational;—No man is rational.

Contradictories.—Two propositions are said to be contradictories, when both have the same subject and the same predicate, but when they differ both in quantity and quality, e.g., All men are rational;—Some men are not rational.

We must not confuse contradictory propositions with contradictory terms. Two terms are said to be contradictory when the objects of the ideas which the terms stand for have nothing in common, inasmuch as one of the objects is a 'being of a certain kind' and the other, 'nothing of that certain kind.' The two objects, in other words, belong to two different genera, e.g., Moral and not-moral. A non-moral thing does not belong to the genus, 'human act,' e.g., a stone. A stone belongs to the genus 'material substance.' In the same way we must not confuse contrary propositions with contrary terms. Contrary terms denote an opposition which exists between the two extremes of a series of things belonging to the same genus. For instance if degrees of color (the genus), are mentally represented as a series, the two extremes, black and white, are contraries. Black and white have not an altogether different genus, but a common one, viz.—color, whereas the predicates of two contrary propositions must belong to two different genera, e.g., Men are rational. Men are not rational.

The opposition of contrary terms is likewise understood to be such opposition between the qualities denoted by two terms, as to imply that the qualities—although of the same genus—cannot exist in the same subject at the same time, e.g., sickness and health; justice and injustice; courage and cowardice.

Subalterns.—One proposition is said to be the subaltern of another when it has the same subject, the same predicate and the same quality as another which is universal in quantity, while it is particular in quantity, e.g., All men are rational, Some men are rational.

Sub-Contraries.—Two propositions are said to be sub-contraries when both having the same subject and the same predicate are particular in quantity, but differ in quality, e.g., Some men are rational;—Some men are not rational.

The Laws of Opposition.—The laws of opposition tell us when inferences based upon the relationships between contraries, contradictories, subalterns and sub-contraries are valid and when they are not valid.

The Square of Opposition.—The square of opposition will help us to visualize the four relationships dealt with in inferences by opposition.

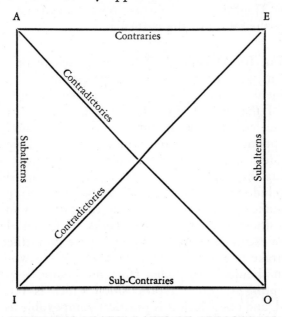

SUMMARY OF THE LAWS OF OPPOSITION
Contraries cannot both be true.
Contraries may both be false.

Contradictories cannot both be true.
Contradictories cannot both be false.

Sub-contraries cannot both be false.
Sub-contraries may both be true.

SUBALTERNS

The truth of the particular follows from truth of the universal.

The falsity of the universal follows from the falsity of the particular.

Hint for Debating.—When in a debate or a discussion, we wish to disprove a proposition which an opponent defends, it is enough to prove the contradictory of that proposition. It is not necessary;—indeed it is not advisable to attempt to prove the contrary of our opponent's contention; it may even be well nigh impossible to do so. If, for example, our opponent is defending the proposition:—"All works of fiction should be excluded from the young;"—in order to refute him, it is sufficient for us to prove the contradictory of that proposition, namely,—"Some works of fiction should not be excluded from the young." If we go farther and undertake to prove too much, namely,—"No works of fiction should be excluded from the young,"—we are attempting to prove a proposition which is very unsound, and one which it is practically impossible as well as ridiculous to uphold.

The fundamental reason why we should not try to refute any universal statement or proposition, by trying to prove its contrary, is this:—contraries may both be false. This is really the case with the example cited in the preceding paragraph.

On the other hand, we should be careful not to err in the opposite direction by proving too little. In order to refute a proposition, universal in quantity, it is not sufficient to establish its subaltern; neither is it sufficient to establish the other sub-contrary, when an opponent's proposition is itself a sub-contrary or in other words, a proposition, 'particular in quantity.' The assertion:—"All works of fiction which teach immorality, should be excluded from the young," is not refuted by establishing the subaltern,—"Some works of fiction which teach immorality, should be excluded from the young." Both propositions, as is obvious, are true. Neither is the assertion:—"Some Catholics are illiterate,"—refuted by establishing its sub-contrary,—"Some Catholics are not illiterate,"—and the reason is: subcontraries may both be true. We succeed in refuting an opponent's propositions, only when we prove that what he contends for is false.

It is always more difficult to refute the contention of an opponent when his contention is expressed as a particular affirmative or a particular negative proposition than when it is expressed as a universal proposition, affirmative or negative, for it is then necessary to prove the contradictory of his assertion, which will in this case, have to be the proof of a universal proposition. It is always more difficult to prove the truth of any universal proposition than to prove the truth of a proposition, particular in quantity.

To win a debate it is not necessary to prove that what our opponent is contending for is false. All that is necessary is to show he is not proving his point.

CONVERSION OF PROPOSITIONS

Simple Conversion of Propositions.—Simple conversion of propositions is another species of immediate inference,—another act or operation of the mind by which from one proposition, (the convertend), we immediately infer another proposition, (the converse), of the same quantity and quality by simply interchanging the subject and the predicate of the given proposition. Only E and I propositions can be converted simply.

The Two Rules for Simple Conversion.—Rule 1.— No term may be distributed in the converse which was not distributed in the convertend. Rule 2.—The converse must be the same in quality as the convertend.

The 'convertend' is the proposition which is to be converted.

The 'converse' is the converted proposition.

A term is 'distributed' when it is universal in quantity, (extension).

Simple Conversion of Universal Affirmatives is Invalid.—Universal affirmatives cannot be converted simply, because to convert them simply would involve a violation of rule 1. For example, The converse of:— "All trees are plants" would be:—"All plants are trees." In the converted proposition, 'plants' is universal in quantity, whereas in the convertend, it was particular in quantity, because it was the predicate of an affirmative proposition.

Conversion 'Per Accidens'.—Universal affirmative propositions may be converted 'per accidens.' A conversion of a universal proposition 'per accidens' is a conversion in which we preserve both the quality of the original proposition as well as the quantity of the particular predicate term of the convertend, when it becomes the subject term of the converse. The original quantity of the predicate term of the convertend is preserved in the converse when we qualify it in the converse by the word, 'some' in place of the term, 'all.' Since E propositions can be converted simply there is not any advantage in converting them 'per accidens'.

Conversion of Universal Negatives.—Universal negative propositions may be converted simply, and the reason is:—a conversion of a universal negative does not involve any violation of either of the two rules for the simple conversion of propositions. In particular, there is no change of quantity involved, with either the subject or predicate term in the conversion of a universal negative, e.g., No man is an angel; therefore, no angel is a man.

Conversion of Particular Affirmatives.—Particular affirmative propositions can likewise be converted simply for the same reason that in the conversion of particular affirmatives, there is no change of quantity of either the subject or the predicate in the converted proposition, e.g., Some roses are red;—therefore, Some red things are roses.

Conversion of Particular Negatives is Invalid.—By analyzing a particular negative proposition it can be

readily seen that its conversion is invalid. For example:
—Some roses are not red, cannot be validly converted
into:—Some red things are not roses, because the term,
'roses' as the subject of the convertend is particular in
quantity, but as the predicate of the converse it has to
become universal in quantity. The predicate of every
negative proposition is universal in quantity, or, as it is
expressed, it is 'distributed.'

Obversion and Contraposition.*—Particular negative propositions can be obverted, and then if it is desired, the obverted proposition can be simply converted.
The converted form of an obverted proposition is the
contraposited form of the original proposition, i.e., of
the proposition before it was obverted. A, E, I, and O
propositions may be obverted.

Definition of Obversion.—Obversion is that process
of immediate reasoning by which from a given proposition, we infer another of the same quantity, but of different quality from the given proposition; having for
its subject, the subject of the given proposition; and
for its predicate, the contradictory of the predicate of
the given or original proposition.

Definition of Contraposition.—Contraposition is a
process of immediate inference in which from a given
proposition we infer another, of different quality; hav-

---

* Obversion and contraposition are treated by many logicians not so
much as species of immediate reasoning but as methods of expressing any
given propositions in other propositional forms which are equivalent in
meaning to the propositions as given in the original forms. For this reason obversion and contraposition are explained in many logic texts under
the heading of 'equivalence or equipollence.' This is not to say, however,
that these processes may not be treated as species of immediate inference.

ing for its subject, the contradictory of the predicate and for predicate the subject of the original proposition. Only 'A' and 'O' propositions can be contraposited. If we start to contraposit an 'E' or an 'I' proposition we get by obversion an 'A' or 'O' proposition respectively. The process must end there as the latter propositions cannot be converted simply. In effect, contraposition is the simple conversion of any obverted proposition.

Examples to Show the Process of Obversion and the Process of Contraposition.—Some lawyers are not honest.—1. Change the quality of this proposition and we have, Some lawyers are honest.—2. Substitute for the predicate of the given proposition its contradictory and the result is: Some lawyers are dishonest, which is the obverted form of the given proposition.

If now, the obverted form of 'Some lawyers are not honest' is converted simply, the result is, 'Some dishonest men are lawyers,' which is the contraposited form of the original proposition, 'Some lawyers are not honest.'

Contradictories of Terms.—As stated before, a contradictory of a term must not be confused with a contradictory of a proposition. (See text, p. 61.) The contradictory of a term is the same term modified by the negative, 'not.' Now it is customary in English to substitute in the case of many terms, the prefixes 'un', 'in', 'im' etc., for the negative 'not' and to consider a term thus prefixed, as the contradictory of the term without the prefix. Strictly speaking such prefixed terms are not the contradictory but the contrary of the term without the prefix. The contradictory of 'scrupulous,' e.g., is 'not-scrupulous:'—unscrupulous is the contrary. 'Not-justice' is the contradictory: 'injustice' is the contrary of 'justice'. There is a difference in the meaning of the two terms. Seeing a group of boys playing ball, I would not say of them that they are doing an act of injustice and yet what they are doing is an act which is 'not-justice', i.e., the act of playing ball is not of the same genus as the act of justice; it is, 'being' of a different kind. Similarly to say a man is 'not-scrupulous' is a different thing from saying, 'he is unscrupulous.' So general, however, is this inexact use of the contrary for the contradictory in writing the obverted form of a term, that it would seem we need not be too meticulous about the error unless the difference in meaning between a word written with the negative 'not' and a word written with the prefix 'un', 'in', etc. is of considerable importance, as, e.g., is the case with 'scrupulous' and 'unscrupulous.'

The following remark of Newman in "The Grammar of Assent," p. 47, seems to be authority enough for the assertion made at the end of the foregoing paragraph.

"Hence in science we sometimes use a definition or a formula, not as exact, but as being sufficient for our purpose, for working out certain conclusions, for a practical approximation, the error being small, till a certain point is reached."

Added Determinants.—If in algebra we are warranted in inferring that because A equals B;—then A plus X equals B plus X, even so, in Logic, if we add a definite qualifying word to the subject of a proposition, the qualified subject ought to be equal to the predicate of the proposition when qualified by the same word.

For example, If, 'All negroes are men,' it ought to follow that:—'All honest negroes are honest men.'

This process of immediate inference just described is called: 'inference by added deterinants.' 'Added determinants' is a process of immediate inference, therefore, in which from a given proposition we infer another by limiting or qualifying both the subject and the predicate of the original proposition by the same word or term. Sometimes an inference according to added determinants is valid; sometimes it is not.

In order to make sure of avoiding false inference when inferring according to this method; (1) Make sure that the added determinant is not merely a relative term, as: 'large,' 'small' and the like; (2) Recall the variety of meanings the added determinant may have and see if it qualifies the subject and predicate in exactly the same way. Many adjectives may qualify the subject in one way and the predicate in an entirely different way.

QUESTIONS FOR REVIEW

1. Define immediate inference.
2. Define opposition.
3. When are two propositions said to be contraries? contradictories? subalterns? sub-contraries?
4. Summarize the laws of 'opposition.'
5. What proposition must be established in order to refute an opponent in debate? Give the reason for your answer.
6. What is meant by the conversion of propositions?
7. Define the 'convertend' and the 'converse.'
8. State the two essential rules for the valid simple conversion of a proposition.

9. What is conversion of a proposition 'per accidens?'
10. Explain why an 'universal affirmative' proposition cannot be validly converted by simple conversion.
11. What two types of propositions can be validly converted?
12. Prove that particular negative propositions cannot be validly converted.
13. Explain the process of obversion.
14. Define obversion.
15. Define contraposition. Show the process of contraposition by an example.
16. Explain what is meant by the process of immediate inference called 'added determinants.'
17. State what two precautions must be remembered in order to make a valid inference according to the method of 'added determinants.'

EXERCISES IN OPPOSITION, OBVERSION, CONTRAPOSITION AND IN THE CONVERSION OF PROPOSITIONS.—VALID AND INVALID EXAMPLES OF ADDED DETERMINANTS.

1. If "A" is true, what is: "O"—"E"—"I"?
2. If "A" is false, what is: "O"—"E"—"I"?
3. If "E" is true, what is: "I"—"A"—"O"?
4. If "E" is false, what is: "I"—"A"—"O"?
5. If "I" is true, what is: "E"—"A"—"O"?
6. If "I" is false, what is: "E"—"A"—"O"?
7. If "O" is true, what is: "A"—"E"—"I"?
8. If "O" is false, what is: "A"—"I"—"E"?

*   *   *   *

Give the contrary (or sub-contrary), and the contradictory of:
1. All metals are elements.
2. No coward need apply.*

---

* What is the real meaning of the term, 'need' in this statement?

3. Socrates was the wisest man in Athens.
4. Not all men are brave.
5. No man but a traitor would have done this.
6. Roses do not grow on thistles.
7. All philosophy begins in wonder.
8. Marco Polo was an explorer.

* * * *

According to 'inference by opposition,' give the three other possible propositions which may be inferred from each of the following propositions. Determine the truth or falsity of each inferred proposition.

Given as true:

1. All cats are felines.
2. Some soils are not productive.
3. Eye glasses may do more harm than good.
4. No alcoholic liquor may be sold in the U. S.
5. All continents have primary axes.
6. No criminal is really successful.
7. Not all politicians are dishonest.
8. Only some citizens have the right to vote.

Given as false:

1. No alcohol is sold in the U. S.
2. Some presidents of the U. S. have served three terms.
3. All reputable scientists admit Evolution as a proven fact.
4. Laborers do not deserve wages above the margin of subsistence.
5. All men desire wealth.
6. Only philosophers fail to see the difference between a post and the idea of a post.

* * * *

What is the simplest proposition which must be established in order to disprove the following statements:

1. No man is perfectly happy.

2. Some knowledge is not of any value.
3. All men desire wealth.
4. All works of fiction should be removed from public libraries.
5. Haste makes waste.
6. The burnt child dreads the fire.

*   *   *   *

Test the following propositions. Are all of them properly obverted?

1. These lawyers are all truthful.
   None of these lawyers are untruthful.
2. No man is immortal.
   All men are mortal.
3. Some business men are honest.
   Some business men are not dishonest.
4. Some chemical compounds are stable.
   Some chemical compounds are not unstable.
5. These students are all active.
   None of these students are inactive.
6. These apples are all ripe.
   None of these apples are unripe.
7. Some beverages are healthful.
   Some beverages are not unhealthful.
8. Some houses are comfortable.
   Some houses are not uncomfortable.
9. All men are rational.
   No man is irrational.
10. Some students are not wise.
    Some students are unwise.
11. Some surgeons are skillful.
    Some surgeons are not skillful.

12.   These students are all fit to play basketball.
      None of these students are unfit to play basketball.
13.   The speakers are all deserving of credit.
      None of the speakers is undeserving of credit.
14.   All crimes are voluntary.
      No crime is involuntary.
15.   All probable events are possible.
      No probable event is impossible.
16.   A man who is all thumbs is unhandy.
      No man who is all thumbs is handy.
17.   I shall not all die.
      I am not one who shall all die.
18.   A few are ever true to their tasks.
      A few are not ever untrue to their tasks.

*   *   *   *

Test these examples in contraposition:

1.   All men are mortal.
     Nothing immortal is a man.

     All men are mortal.
     No man is immortal.
     Nothing immortal is a man.

2.   All men are rational.
     Nothing irrational is a man.
     All men are rational.
     No man is irrational.
     Nothing irrational is a man.

3.   Some animals are not vertebrates.
     Some invertebrates are animals.

     Some animals are not vertebrates.
     Some animals are invertebrates.

4. The voluntary muscles are all striped.
   No unstriped muscles are voluntary.

   The voluntary muscles are all striped.
   No voluntary muscles are unstriped.
   No unstriped muscles are voluntary.

5. Unstriped muscles are all involuntary.
   No voluntary muscles are unstriped.

   Unstriped muscles are all involuntary.
   No unstriped muscles are voluntary.
   No voluntary muscles are unstriped.

6. All wise acts are honest acts.
   No dishonest act is a wise act.

   All wise acts are honest acts.
   No wise act is a dishonest act.
   No dishonest act is a wise act.

7. Every candid man avows his mistake.
   No one who disavows his mistake is a candid man.

   Every candid man avows his mistake.
   No candid man disavows his mistake.
   No one who disavows his mistake is a candid man.

8. All metals are elements.
   No non-element is a metal.

9. All civilized peoples are progressive.
   No unprogressive people is civilized.

10. All material things are extended.
    No inextended thing is material.

11. All rights are inextended.
    Nothing extended is a right.

12. Some liquids are not healthful.
    Some unhealthful things are liquids.

State the relation between:

1. Good men are wise.

2. Unwise men are not good.

3. Some unwise men are good.

4. No good men are unwise.

*   *   *   *

Criticise the following:—

Granted that it is true that:

> All wise men are mortal; then,
> No wise men are immortal; and
> No immortal beings are wise men.

Hence it is false that:

> Some immortal beings are wise men; and that,
> Some immortal beings are not wise men.

But if this is false, it must be true that:

> All immortal beings are not unwise men; and that,
> Some unwise men are immortal beings;
> Some wise men are not immortal beings. *(Quoted from Sellars.)*

*   *   *   *

State the logical process by which we pass from each of the following propositions to the succeeding one:

1. All metals are elements.

2. No metals are non-elements.

3. No non-elements are metals.

4. All non-elements are non-metals.

5. All metals are elements.

6. Some elements are metals.

7. Some metals are elements.—*Jevons.*

ADDED DETERMINANTS

Which of the following inferences are valid?

1. Hottentots are men.
   A clever Hottentot is a clever man.
2. An elephant is an animal.
   A small elephant is a small animal.
3. The army is worn out with fatigue.
   Half the army is half worn out with fatigue.
4. Judges are lawyers.
   A majority of judges is a majority of lawyers.
5. A sheep is not a dog.
   The owner of a sheep is not the owner of a dog.

CHAPTER VI

THE LOGIC OF MEDIATE REASONING

Kinds of Inference.—Inference has already been described as that act or operation of the mind by which a judgment implicitly contained in one or more propositions called the 'premise,' or 'premises,' is brought out explicitly in a new proposition, called the 'conclusion.' When there is no more than one premise expressed or implied, the process of reasoning is called immediate inference: when there are two or more premises, the process of reasoning is called mediate inference or mediate reasoning.

When in the process of reasoning, we proceed from the more general to the less general truths, the mode of reasoning is called deductive reasoning. When we proceed from the less general to the more general, the process of reasoning is called inductive reasoning. The most common form for the expression of deductive reasoning is the SYLLOGISM.

The Syllogism.—The syllogism may be defined as that form of expressing an instance of mediate inference which is used when we proceed to bring out explicitly in a third proposition, a judgment which was implicitly contained in the relationship of two preceding propositions. For example:—All flowers are plants; The rose is a flower; therefore, the rose is a plant.

Elements of the Syllogism.—The first two propositions of the syllogism are called the premises; the third, —the conclusion.

If we examine the premises and the conclusion more closely, we shall find that there are three and only three different terms in the syllogism. We shall further notice that one of the three terms occurs twice, i.e., once in each premise,—but not in the conclusion. It never should. This term which occurs twice in the premises is called 'the middle term.' Of the other two terms, the term which appears as the 'subject' of the conclusion, is called 'the minor term;' the other, which appears as the predicate of the conclusion, is called 'the major term.' The premise which contains 'the major term' is 'the major premise,' and the premise which contains 'the minor term,' is called the 'minor premise.'

The vital thing in a syllogism is the conclusive force, the convincing power, the consequence which every valid syllogism has. He who assents to the premises of a valid syllogism, is carried on by the nature of the human mind to assent to the conclusion which follows from those premises.

The Inclusive Method.—Reading the propositions according to 'extension' is the mode followed in this book. The cogency of this method may be explained as follows: According to this method, if we take the simple example quoted above—'All flowers are plants;'— 'The rose is a flower;'—therefore, 'The rose is a plant;'—we find that in a typical syllogism, there is a larger class — (plants) — represented by the major term; a smaller class—(flowers)—represented by the middle term, and a smallest class—(roses)—represented by the minor term. The conclusion is affirmed in virtue of the relation between the three classes, for whatever is affirmed or denied in the same sense of any class, may be affirmed or denied of each member of that class. This is the celebrated "Dictum de Omni et Nullo." It is Aristotle's axiom. It is an abbreviated expression of two axioms: "Dictum de Omni"—"Dictum de Nullo." The full meaning of the two axioms is: Whatever may be predicated of a whole class, may be predicated of each member of that class,—and—whatever may be denied of a whole class, may be denied of each member of that class.

There are eight rules derived from this dictum of Aristotle, which if perfectly mastered, are sufficient to guide us in constructing valid syllogisms.

N.B. A syllogism, valid in form, gives objective logical truth in the conclusion only when the premises are objectively true. Test premises for objective logical truth according to the important rule in Chapter Four, if they are not obviously objectively true.

RULES OF THE SYLLOGISM

1. A syllogism must have three, and only three terms. This rule is based on the very nature of the syllogism. The first term, is, 'whatever is predicated;' the second term, is 'the class-concept of which it is predicated;' and the third term; is, 'what is asserted to belong to that class.' For example, 'Horses are quadrupeds'—'Dexter is a horse'—'Dexter is a quadruped.' 'Quadrupeds' is, 'whatever is predicated';—'horse' is 'the class-concept' of which it is predicated;—'Dexter' is asserted to belong to that class. We predicate quadrupeds of the whole

class of horses; Dexter is one of them. Therefore, we predicate quadruped of Dexter.

2. A syllogism must have three and only three propositions. This rule, again, is based upon the very nature of the syllogism. One of the propositions may be suppressed, but it should be capable of being expressed.

N.B.—These first two rules of structure are not properly speaking, rules, but rather a statement of the essential requirements of the very nature of the syllogism.

3. The 'middle term' must be distributed—(used in its full extension or in the universal sense)—in one at least, of the premises. The reason of this rule is easily seen. If it is not distributed, but used in both premises indefinitely, or in the particular sense;—(as if in the example above, we should substitute 'some horses'),—we could not be sure that the two other terms or the two extremes, were not being compared with entirely different portions of the extension of the middle term. One of the other terms might be compared with one portion, and the other term with another portion of the indefinite 'some' of the 'middle term.' We can draw no conclusions about the relation between the two extreme terms unless we are sure of having compared each of these with exactly the same portion of the 'middle term.' This is only possible when the 'middle term' is used at least once in the 'universal sense.'

4. No term may be distributed in the conclusion which was not distributed in the premise in which it occurred. We cannot go beyond our data. We cannot take more out of our premises than we put into them. We cannot, therefore, take a term in the conclusion,

more widely than in the premises. When 'the major term' is taken more widely in the conclusion than in the premise, the logical fallacy is called: 'the illicit process of the major.' When the 'minor term' is taken more widely in the conclusion than in the premise, the logical fallacy is called: 'the illicit process of the minor.'

5.   If one of the premises is negative, the conclusion must be negative. The validity of this rule is again easily seen, for if one of two things disagrees with a third, and the other agrees with this same third, the two cannot agree with each other.

6.   From two negative propositions, no conclusion can be drawn. If both extreme terms are declared to be unconnected with the common 'middle term,' how can we compare them with each other at all?

N.B.—This rule does not state simply and absolutely that from two propositions which are negative in form, nothing can follow, but that no inference may be drawn about either of two extremes from comparing these in two really negative judgments with a single third term.

7.   From two particular propositions, no conclusion can be drawn.

8.   If one premise is particular, the conclusion must be particular.*

---

* The perfect syllogism is that in which the 'middle term' appears as the subject of the 'major,' and the predicate of the 'minor premise.' Such things as 'moods' and 'figures' of the syllogism and the 'reduction' of other forms to the perfect form of the syllogism, as not being absolutely necessary to the right understanding of syllogistic reasoning, will not be treated in this book. The rules of the syllogism, thoroughly mastered, is all that is necessary for correct reasoning according to syllogistic form. We have omitted the explanation of 'moods' and 'figures,' therefore, as superfluous in an 'Outline of Logic.'

The Enthymeme.—A syllogism is seldom expressed in its complete form except in the most formal discourse or written argumentation. Usually one premise or the conclusion is understood, i.e., implied, and not expressed in language. The enthymeme, is a form of mediate inference;—in substance, a syllogism which suppresses one of the premises or the conclusion.

An argument is easily recognized as an enthymeme, when it consists of only two statements, one of which begins with or is expressed with the word, 'therefore.' Secondly, whenever in an argument consisting of only two statements the words: 'because'—'for'—or—'since' occur, we may look for an enthymeme. Finally, whenever we attribute any quality or characteristic to a class of things, and then add that a particular person or thing belongs to the class in question, we have an enthymeme.

When the enthymeme is of the type which suppresses one of the premises, the subject of the conclusion given, is the 'minor,' while the predicate of the conclusion given, is the 'major' term of the syllogism which might be evolved from the enthymeme. Moreover, the 'middle term' is at hand in the one premise given. Knowing the three terms, it becomes an easy thing to state in full, the syllogism of which any particular enthymeme of the type referred to, is a part.

When the enthymeme is of the type in which the conclusion is suppressed, it is a simple matter, likewise, to state the syllogism of which the enthymeme is a part. For with the two premises given, the term which occurs twice, will be the 'middle term' of this syllogism, and all that remains to be done is to combine the other two terms into a proposition affirmative or negative as the case demands, for the conclusion of the syllogism, and taking care that neither term has a greater quantity in the conclusion than in the premise.

The enthymeme is a tricky form of argument, and the surest way of detecting the weakness or the flaw in it, is to proceed at once to formulate it in a syllogism.

Criticizing an Enthymeme.—Any form of reasoning may be put in the form of an enthymeme. In criticizing an enthymeme we must attend not only to what is said, but also to what is left unsaid. What is left unsaid is likely to escape notice. We must always be careful to examine whether the unexpressed premise is objectively true or not. Volumes have been written for instance, to urge the adoption of the 'direct primary' for the selection of candidates for office, because the 'direct primary' would be a means of arousing the interest of the voters in matters of government. This reasoning implies the general principle that, "whatever means will ensure the interest of the voters in the government" should be adopted. Such reasoning does not lead to a true conclusion unless the general principle referred to, is true. Suppressed majors contain general principles. He who is reasoning through the form of an enthymeme rightly or wrongly, assumes that the principles suppressed are accepted by all, and centers all his efforts on the minor premise.

If the implied general principle then, is not objectively true, and especially if it cannot be approved of on moral grounds, the conclusion that is drawn from it is not true and cannot be accepted. The danger with enthymemes is one which arises from 'logical falsity.' The suppressed principle of an enthymeme is generally void of 'objective logical truth.' Hence always test the suppressed premise of an enthymeme by the important rule, (Chapter Four).

The Aristotelian Sorites.—The Aristotelian sorites is a form of argument consisting of three or more premises, and one conclusion following from them. The conclusion of an Aristotelian sorites is always made up of the subject of the first premise and the predicate of the last premise.

For example:

He who desponds ceases to labor;
He who ceases to labor makes no progress;
(. . . . .)
He who makes no progress does not reach the end;
He who desponds does not reach the end.

Analyses of the Aristotelian Sorites.—Notice in the example above, that the conclusion from the first two premises was suppressed, as indicated by the marks (. . . . . .). That is the nature of the Aristotelian sorites. It abbreviates by dropping intermediate conclusions. It presumes the evidence of the conclusion after the first two premises. Instead of explicitly giving the conclusion of the first two premises, it proceeds to add a third premise. Notice, that the predicate of the second premise, becomes the subject of the third, but the predicate of the third is an altogether new predicate. In this way the Aristotelian sorites might proceed to pile up premises indefinitely. To close or conclude an Aristotelian sorites, make the subject of the first premise the subject of the final conclusion; the predicate of this conclusion will be the predicate of the last premise.

This is the Aristotelian sorites. It may be defined, then, as a series of propositions so arranged that the predicate of the first becomes the subject of the second, with another new predicate attributed to it; the predicate of the second, the subject of the third, with another new predicate attributed to it; and so on, until finally, the subject of the first and the predicate of the last premise are united to form the conclusion.

Example of an Aristotelian Sorites.—"Where human selfishness is allowed to rule the actions of men, human justice is very soon lost sight of. Where justice is lost sight of, honesty is little practiced. Where honesty is little practiced, confidence is destroyed. Where confidence is destroyed, suspicion, distrust, and consequent unrest always follow. (That is just what has happened.) The selfishness and unconscionable greed in the world today has been productive of a seething mass of discontent and unrest (that makes thoughtful men everywhere fearful of the consequence that may follow.)"*

The Polysyllogism.—In the first place the polysyllogism is a chain of reasoning like the sorites. But whereas the sorites suppresses the conclusion from its first two premises, the polysyllogism expresses it. That is the first difference. This conclusion of the first syllogism is now considered as a premise of a second syllogism; similarly the conclusion of the second syllogism will be a premise of the third syllogism. The polysyllogism then may proceed indefinitely in this way, unlike

---

* Parts in parentheses are not parts of the form.

the sorites, by piling up syllogisms instead of premises. The sorites finally unites the subject of the first premise with the predicate of the last for the conclusion, but the polysyllogism does not reach back to its first premise for its subject of its final conclusion.

A polysyllogism is, therefore, a chain of syllogisms in which the conclusion of the preceding syllogism is made a premise of the succeeding one.

Example of a Polysyllogism.—No simple substance can be dissolved into parts; all spiritual substances are simple; therefore, no spiritual substance can be dissolved into parts. The soul is a spiritual substance; therefore, it cannot be dissolved. What cannot be dissolved is immortal; therefore, the soul is immortal.

The Epichireme.—The epichireme is a syllogism containing besides the two premises, the proof or part of the proof of one of the premises. For example:

Whatever is spiritual is immortal—because it is incapable of corruption.

The human soul is spiritual.

Therefore, the human soul is immortal.

EXAMPLES OF FALSE SYLLOGISMS

1. Beings that are not free are incapable of sin.
   Slaves are beings that are not free.
   Slaves are incapable of sin.   Four Terms.
2. Animal is a genus.
   A tiger is an animal.
   A tiger is a genus.   Four Terms.

3. A cat is a carnivorous animal.
   Carnivorous animals do not eat grains.
   Man does not eat grains.
   Man is not a carnivorous animal.   Four Propositions.

4. All birds are vertebrates.
   All fishes are vertebrates.
   All fishes are birds.   Undistributed Middle.

5. All men are beings with an immortal destiny.
   Brutes are not men.
   Brutes are not beings with an immortal destiny.
                            Illicit Process of Major.

6. All men are animals.
   Brutes are not men.
   Brutes are not animals.   Illicit Process of Major.

7. All witty men are dreaded.
   All witty men are admired.
   All who are admired are dreaded.
                            Illicit Process of Minor.

8. What is not metallic is not magnetic.
   Carbon is not-metallic.
   Carbon is not magnetic.   Two Apparent Negatives.
                               (Why only apparent?)

9. Some terms are clear.
   Some ideas are expressed in terms.
   Some ideas are clear.   Two Particulars. Four Terms.

10. Some men are Chinese.
    Some Asiatics are not Chinese.
    Some Asiatics are not men.   Illicit Process of Major.

11. Some slaves are not happy.
    No slaves are free.
    Some beings that are free are not happy.
                                     Two Negatives.

12. All gold is precious.
    All gold is a mineral.
    Every mineral is precious.   Illicit Process of Minor.

13. All criminal actions are punishable by law.
    Prosecution for theft is a criminal action.
    Therefore prosecution for theft is punishable by law.

                                                    Four Terms.

14. One who habitually violates a law is a dangerous person.
    One who habitually uses four terms in a syllogism habitually violates a law.
    Therefore one who habitually uses four terms in a syllogism is a dangerous person.   Four Terms.

15. All civilized men eat cooked food.
    All civilized men wear clothes.
    Therefore all who wear clothes eat cooked food.

                                        Illicit Process of Minor.

16. Some pagans are virtuous.
    No robbers are virtuous.
    No robbers are pagans.   Illicit Process of Major.

17. No mosquitoes are agreeable.
    All mosquitoes buzz.
    No buzzing things are agreeable.

                                        Illicit Process of Minor.

*   *   *   *

In the following Syllogisms: (a) Distinguish the middle, major, and minor terms. (b) State why each of the syllogisms is invalid in form.

1. No squares are circles.
   No triangles are circles.
   No triangles are squares.

2. All Virginians are Americans.
   Some Americans are Negroes.
   Some Negroes are Virginians.

   illicit major

3. No elements are compounds.
   Gold is not an element.
   Gold is not compound.

   2 neg

4. All churches have crosses on their steeples.
   This building has a cross on its steeple.
   This building is a church.

   illicit major

5. No vegetable has a heart.
   A good lettuce has a heart.
   A good lettuce is not a vegetable.

   4 terms

6. The wise are good.
   Some ignorant people are good.
   Some ignorant people are wise.

   4 terms

7. Some sweetmeats are unwholesome.
   No beverages are sweetmeats.
   No beverages are unwholesome.

   illicit major

8. Some pagans are virtuous.
   No housebreakers are virtuous.
   Some housebreakers are not pagans.

   illicit major

9. No tyrants are friends to liberty.
   Some statesmen are not friends to liberty.
   Some statesmen are tyrants.

   2 neg

10. All swans are said to sing before they die.
    Some waterfowl are swans.
    All waterfowl sing before they die.

    illicit minor

11. Some union men are Democrats.
    Some union men are carpenters.
    Some carpenters are Democrats.

    2 part

12. Some rocks are sedimentary.

No granites are sedimentary.
Granites are not rocks.

13. All Parisians are Frenchmen.
Some artists are Frenchmen.
Some artists are Parisians.

14. Metals are conductors of electricity.
The atmosphere is not a metal.
The atmosphere is not a conductor of electricity.

15. Whatever is opposed to our industrial prosperity is a serious evil.
All European wars are serious evils.
All European wars are opposed to our industrial prosperity.

16. All great talkers are wearisome to their friends.
No silent men are great talkers.
No silent men are wearisome to their friends.

17. Some Africans have woolly heads.
All Egyptians are Africans.
All Egyptians have woolly heads.

18. Some taxi drivers are impolite.
Some gentlemen are taxi drivers.
Some gentlemen are impolite.

19. All sheep are graminivorous.
Horses are not sheep.
Horses are not graminivorous.

20. All lemons are sour.
All unripe fruits are sour.
All lemons are unripe fruit.

21. All oysters are nutritious.
No oysters are in season in July.
Some things not in season in July are not nutritious.

22. All men are beings with an immortal destiny.

Brutes are not men.
Brutes are not beings with an immortal destiny.

23. All birds are vertebrates.
All fishes are vertebrates.
All fishes are birds.

24. No sweetmeats are unwholesome.
Beverages are not sweetmeats.
Beverages are not unwholesome.

25. All witty men are dreaded.
All witty men are admired.
All who are admired are dreaded.

26. All men are animals.
Brutes are not men.
Brutes are not animals.

* * * *

EXERCISES IN SYLLOGIZING

(a) Arrange in syllogistic form: (b) Determine whether the syllogism is valid, and secondly, whether it expresses objective truth. If not, why not?*

* Before attempting to complete a syllogism from an enthymeme or before arranging any statements or propositions in syllogistic form; first, make certain of what the speaker or writer of the enthymeme or the statement, is trying to persuade or convince you, or of what he is simply trying to tell you. What he is trying to tell you will be the conclusion of the syllogism to be arranged. The predicate of the conclusion will also be the predicate of the major premise of the syllogism (premise No. 1), and the subject of the conclusion of the syllogism will be the subject of the minor premise (premise No. 2). All that then remains to be done is to express the middle term as the subject of the major, universalizing it, i.e., modifying it by some such words as: all, every, no, none,—and then expressing it as the predicate of the minor premise. Lo, you have your syllogism. The major or minor premise must be a negative, if the conclusion is negative. Arrange both premises and the conclusion in logical form. If a valid syllogism cannot be developed from the material given in any non-syllogistic arguments, it is proof that the non-syllogistic argument is neither valid nor a good argument.

1. He is not indifferent to money, for he is a sensible man, and no sensible man despises money.

2. All human productions are liable to error, and therefore all books being human productions are liable to error.

3. No man desires pain, and without pain your friend's cure is impossible; therefore, he will not desire to be cured.

4. Englishmen admire all who are successful; they must, therefore, admire some persons who are politically dangerous, for assuredly there are some successful persons who are politically dangerous.

5. Gold is not a compound substance, for it is a metal and none of the metals are compounds.

6. A classical education is worthless, for we make no use of the ancient languages in later life.

7. More books are written directly after a war for freedom than at any other time because people are then vitalized by a more active contact with the minds of others.

8. Restless nations are not progressive for we see that all the civilized nations are progressive, while all uncivilized nations are restless.

*   *   *   *

Supply premises for the following conclusions:

1. Some politicians are not dishonest.*

2. The moon tends to fall to the earth.

3. Banks sometimes fail.

4. Some logicians are not good reasoners.

5. No knowledge is useless.

6. Caterpillars are not worms.

*   *   *   *

---

*Ask yourself: What kind of politicians are or are not dishonest? What things tend to fall to the earth, etc.?

Convert the following enthymemes into complete syllogisms; and then criticize the syllogisms for validity and truth.

1. None but material bodies gravitate, therefore, air is a material body.*

2. Copper is a metal; therefore, it conducts electricity.

3. Good soldiers obey orders: he is not a good soldier.

4. Lightning will not strike here because it never strikes twice in the same spot.

5. Only the good are fit to die; and therefore, capital punishment is wrong.

6. He has been a politician for years; he is therefore, not to be trusted.

7. He blushes; therefore, he is guilty.

8. Blessed are the clean of heart, for they shall see God.

9. John is successful and all successful men are intelligent.

10. All liquids flow; this tar will flow.

11. The world displays a wonderful adaptation of means to an end; therefore, it is the work of an intelligent maker.

12. Caesar says (in Shakespeare):
    "Yon Cassius has a lean and hungry look; such men are dangerous."

13. I know he is intoxicated because of the unsteadiness of his gait.

14. Murderers tremble in the presence of the corpse of the murdered man; therefore, we see that this man is a murderer.

15. The use of poison gas in warfare is an effective means of winning a war; therefore, it should be approved.

---

*When dealing with exponable propositions, recall how they must be resolved into two or more simple propositions before they can be dealt with in Logic. Only one or the other simple proposition will be necessary as one from which to build up a syllogism. Choose that one which will give the conclusion desired.

16. The sterilization of morons would check race degeneration; therefore, the practice of sterilization of morons should be adopted.

17. Sometimes nothing but a lie will save another's reputation; therefore, in such cases lies must be allowable.

18. Darius has been victor in the Olympic games; therefore, he should receive a crown.

CHAPTER VII

CONDITIONAL AND DISJUNCTIVE SYLLOGISMS

In the first place, let us recall what a conditional proposition is, and what a disjunctive proposition is. A conditional proposition is one which neither affirms nor denies simply or categorically, but one which makes an affirmation or a denial dependently on the truth or on the consistency of another proposition. Every conditional proposition is divided into two parts, into: the antecedent and the consequent. The antecedent is the part which contains the condition—the part expressed with 'if'; the consequent is the part stated simply and categorically, or as may happen, disjunctively. For instance, in the following proposition: 'If he is a Christian, he believes in God,' the consequent is affirmed simply and categorically. In this conditional proposition: 'If this being is an animal, it is either a man or a brute,' the consequent is affirmed categorically but disjunctively.

A disjunctive proposition is one which offers two or more alternative assertions or denials, or in other words, it is a proposition which makes an alternative predication. From their very nature, (as stated before), all disjunctive propositions are affirmative. The negation of alternatives would not give us a disjunctive proposition but two or more simple negative categorical propositions, e.g., Man is neither a plant nor a mineral,—

97

would be equivalent to: Man is not a plant,—Man is not a mineral.

CONDITIONAL SYLLOGISMS

A conditional syllogism is better defined by a genetic definition, i.e., by one which tells how it is constructed. A conditional syllogism then, is one which has for its major premise, a conditional proposition. The minor premise must be a categorical proposition; either an affirmation of the antecedent of the major premise proposition, or a denial of the consequent of the major premise proposition. The conclusion must likewise be a categorical proposition; either an affirmation of the consequent of the major premise proposition, if the minor was an affirmation of its antecedent; or a denial of the antecedent of the major premise proposition, if the minor was a denial of its consequent.*

Rules of the Conditional Syllogism.—The rules of the conditional syllogism have been implicitly stated in the definition of the conditional syllogism just given. They may be explicitly formulated as follows:

Rule 1.—If in the minor premise of a conditional syllogism we affirm the antecedent of the major premise proposition, we may validly affirm the consequent

---

* It must be borne in mind that no inference in a conditional syllogism—even though it is valid in form,—will give a true and certain conclusion unless there is a necessary connection between the antecedent and consequent of the conditional proposition expressed in the major premise. The necessary connection need not be metaphysical; it is sufficient that it be one in accordance either with the physical laws of nature, or one consequent upon the nature of human beings. (See p. 48.)

of the same proposition as the conclusion of the syllogism.

Rule 2.—If in the minor of a conditional syllogism, we deny the consequent of the major premise proposition, we may validly deny the antecedent of the same proposition for the conclusion of the syllogism.

Rule 3.—This rule is a corollary of Rule 1. It is expressed thus: We may not proceed from a denial of the antecedent of the major premise proposition, in the minor, to a denial of the consequent of the major premise proposition for our conclusion.

Rule 4.—This rule is a corollary of Rule 2. It is expressed thus: We may not proceed from an affirmation of the consequent of the major premise proposition, in the minor, to an affirmation of the antecedent of the major premise proposition for our conclusion.*

DISJUNCTIVE SYLLOGISMS

A disjunctive syllogism is one in which the major premise is made up of disjunctive propositions of two or more alternatives; the minor, of a categorical proposition which is either an affirmation or a denial of one or more of the alternatives of the major premise, or which

---

* It is more convenient to employ the term 'posit' to take the place of the term 'affirm.' The antecedent may contain a negative, and in this case, the proposition, in the minor, positing it will also be of a negative quality. To speak of negative propositions as affirmations will cause confusion. Consider the following: If the doctor is not skillful, he will cause the patient much pain. He is not skillful. He will cause the patient much pain. Here we affirm, but better, posit the antecedent by a negative proposition. In the same way, the term 'sublate' may better be used than the term 'deny.'

is an affirmation or a denial of all the alternatives save one. The conclusion is an affirmation of that alternative which was not denied in the minor premise or of all the alternatives which were not denied in the minor; or, vice versa, the conclusion is a denial of that alternative which was not affirmed in the minor, or of all the alternatives which were not affirmed in the minor.

The principle then, on which disjunctive reasoning is based is: the denial of one alternative justifies the affirmation of the other, or the others; the assertion of one alternative justifies the denial of the other or the others.

Rules of Disjunctive Reasoning.—(1) The enumeration of alternatives must be complete.—(2) The alternatives must be mutually exclusive.

Alternatives are mutually exclusive only when it is inconsistent or impossible for the two predicate attributes—(or the three or more if there are more than two)—of the alternatives to be predicated of the subject of the alternatives at the same time.

The practical difficulty in using the disjunctive syllogism arises from the difficulty, amounting sometimes to an impossibility,—of ascertaining whether the enumeration of alternatives is complete and whether the alternatives are mutually exclusive.

The Dilemma.—The force of that form of an argument known as the dilemma, lies in the fact that the argument concludes with a disjunctive proposition of two or more alternatives, either, or any one of which is disagreeable or damaging to an adversary.

The forms of the dilemma are: the complex constructive; and complex destructive dilemma; the simple constructive and the simple destructive.

The nature of a dilemma is best understood from a genetic definition of it, i.e., a definition which details how this form of argument is constructed. The following genetic definition is restricted to the two forms of the dilemma just referred to.

A complex constructive and a complex destructive dilemma has for the major premise two or more conditional propositions. The minor premise consists of a proposition which either disjunctively affirms the antecedents of the propositions stated in the major; or disjunctively denies the consequents of these same propositions. The conclusion is a proposition, which in turn, either disjunctively affirms the consequents of the propositions of the major premise, — if the minor affirmed their antecedents,—and thus we get the complex constructive dilemma, or the conclusion disjunctively denies the antecedents of the propositions of the major—if the minor denied the consequents,—and thus we get the complex destructive dilemma. For example, follow the construction of the following complex constructive dilemma:

If I am going to get well, it is superfluous to call a doctor;
If I am going to die, it is useless to call a doctor;
But, either I am going to get well, or I am going to die;
Therefore, either it is superfluous to call a doctor, or it is useless.

Now follow this example of a complex destructive dilemma:

If Smith were reverent, he would not speak disrespectfully of the Scriptures in earnest;

If he were wise, he would not speak disrespectfully of them in jest;

But either he speaks in earnest or he speaks in jest;

Therefore, Smith is not reverent, or he is not wise.

There are two other forms of the dilemma in use: the one called the simple constructive, and the other called the simple destructive dilemma. Again their nature is best understood by seeing how they are constructed.

The Simple Constructive Dilemma.—In the simple constructive dilemma the major premise consists of two or more conditional propositions, which have different antecedents, but with the consequent, the same for all. The minor is a proposition which disjunctively affirms the antecedents of the propositions found in the major premise. The conclusion is a simple categorical proposition,—the affirmation of the common consequent of the major premise.

Consider this example:

If I go out, I shall catch a cold;

If I stay in, I shall catch a cold;

But either I shall go out, or I shall stay in;

Therefore, I shall catch a cold.

The Simple Destructive Dilemma.*—In the simple destructive dilemma, the major premise consists of two or more conditional propositions which have the same

---

*The simple destructive is not a pure dilemma because the two denials of the minor are not real alternatives.

antecedent for each but with different consequents. The minor is a proposition which denies (?) the several different consequents. The conclusion is a simple categorical proposition, the denial of the common antecedent of the major premise.

An example:

If I am going to be able to pay my rent, I shall have to borrow money;—or—

(If I am going to be able to pay my rent)—I shall have to get to work;

But neither am I able to borrow money, nor am I able to get work;

Therefore, I am not going to be able to pay my rent.

RULES FOR CRITICIZING A DILEMMA

1.—The enumeration of the alternatives in the minor premise must be complete.

2.—In the major, care should be taken that the consequents drawn from the antecedents, and no others really follow from the antecedents. They do not really follow unless there is a necessary connection between the antecedents and the consequents.

3.—A dilemma should be such that it cannot be rebutted. A dilemma is rebutted when the adversary can take the same antecedents in the major and draw consequents opposed to the original consequents, and so establish a conclusion or conclusions to the dilemma, the very opposite of the original conclusion. Thus the advantage is decidedly given to the person who rebuts the original argument, and he is thus given a ready-made weapon that may be used with telling effect.

To Answer a Dilemma.—Show that the antecedents in the major do not necessarily involve the consequents attributed to them; or that the alternatives offered in the disjunctive minor are not completely enumerated; or finally, rebut the proposed dilemma by taking the same antecedents of the major and showing that they involve consequents fatal to the original argument.

EXERCISE

Which of the following conditional syllogisms are valid in form? Which give objective logical truth?

1. If a country is prosperous the people will be loyal;
    The people of this country are loyal;
    The country is prosperous.

2. "If ye were the children of Abraham ye would do the works of Abraham;"
    Ye do not do the works of Abraham;
    Ye are not his children.

3. If he had studied his lesson he would have been able to recite;
    He was able to recite;
    He studied his lesson.

4. If he is a good player he will make the team;
    He is a good player;
    He will make the team.

5. If it becomes colder tonight the pond will be frozen over;
    It will not become colder tonight;
    The pond will not be frozen over.

6. If Caesar was ambitious he deserved to die;
    Caesar deserved to die;
    He was ambitious.

7. If his rifle is damaged he will fail to hit the bull's eye;
   His rifle is not damaged;
   He will not fail to hit the bull's eye.

8. If this novel possesses real literary merit, it will be widely read;
   It will be widely read;
   It possesses real literary merit.

9. If God is infinite in His perfections, He is just;
   He is infinite in His perfections;
   He is just.

10. If the 18th Amendment cannot be enforced, it should be repealed;
    It can be enforced;
    It should be repealed.

11. If he studies he will pass;
    He does not study;
    He will not pass.

12. If a man is honest, he is respected;
    This man is respected;
    He is honest.

13. If a man is honest, he is respected;
    This man is honest; therefore, he is respected;
    This man is not honest; therefore, he is not respected;
    This man is respected; therefore, he is honest;
    This man is not respected; therefore, he is not honest.

14. If a man is not public-spirited, he is not fit to hold office;
    This man is not public-spirited; therefore, he is not fit to hold office;
    This man is public-spirited; therefore, he is fit to hold office;

This man is not fit to hold office; therefore, he is not public-spirited;

This man is fit to hold office; therefore, he is public-spirited.

15. If there is no danger of war, there is no need to prepare for war;
   But there is need to prepare for war;
   Therefore, there is danger of war.

16. If this being is a man, it is a rational animal;
   It is a man; therefore, it is a rational animal;

   It is not a man; therefore, it is not a rational animal;

   It is a rational animal; therefore, it is a man;

   It is not a rational animal; therefore, it is not a man.

17. If this triangle is equilateral, it is equiangular;
   It is equilateral; therefore, it is equiangular;

   It is not equilateral; therefore, it is not equiangular;

   It is equiangular; therefore, it is equilateral;

   It is not equiangular; therefore, it is not equilateral.

*   *   *   *

Determine which of the following Disjunctive Syllogisms are valid, which invalid:

*1. John has either been badly taught or he has himself been lazy and indifferent. But as we know that his teacher is not a man of any learning or ability, we may conclude that John is not to be blamed for his failure.

2. He is either a knave or a fool;
   He is not a knave;
   He is a fool.

---

* Express this example in strict logical form before criticizing it.

3. It is either raining or it is not raining;
   It is not raining;
   It is raining.

4. In order to move, a body must move either in the place where it is or in the place where it is not. But it cannot move in the place where it is, since that place is already occupied. Neither can it move in the place where it is not. Motion, therefore, is impossible.

5. He is either a Frenchman, or an Italian, or a Spaniard;
   He is not a Frenchman or an Italian;
   He is a Spaniard.

6. All triangles are either plane or spherical;
   This triangle is plane; therefore, it is not spherical;

   This triangle is not plane; therefore, it is spherical;

   This triangle is spherical; therefore, it is not plane;

   This triangle is not spherical; therefore, it is plane.

7. All judgments are either analytical or synthetic;
   This judgment is not synthetic; therefore ?

   This judgment is synthetic; therefore ?

8. All propositions are either universal, collective, particular, or singular;

   This judgment is particular; therefore, it is not universal, singular or collective;

   This judgment is not particular; therefore, it is either universal, singular or collective;
   This judgment is not universal, collective or singular; therefore, it is particular.

9. All the inhabitants of this country are either whites or negroes;
   This inhabitant is not white; therefore, he is a negro.

10. Everyone who becomes rich acquires his money by trade or by speculation;

   This man did not acquire his money by trade;

   Therefore, he acquired it by speculation.

11. This man who was drowned was either murdered or committed suicide;

   He did not commit suicide;

   Therefore, he was murdered.

12. Either a triangle has three sides or it has three angles;

   This triangle has three sides;

   Therefore, it has not three angles.

13. The accused is either entirely blameless or altogether guilty;

   He is not entirely blameless;

   Therefore, he is altogether guilty.

*   *   *   *

Answer, if possible, the following dilemmas in any of the three ways convenient and effective:

1. Empson, the notorious agent of Henry VII., is said to have always been able to prove that his victim was capable of paying a large amount of taxes to the king by the following:

   If the accused lives at a small rate, his saving must have made him very rich: if on the other hand, he maintains a large household, his expenditures prove him to be wealthy. But either he lives at a small rate, or he maintains a large expenditure. Therefore, he is rich and consequently can pay heavy taxes to the king.

2. Tertullian's argument against Marcus Aurelius:

   Either the Christians have committed crimes or they have not. If they have committed crimes, your refusal to permit a public inquiry is irrational. If they have committed no offense, it is unjust to punish them. Your conduct, therefore, Marcus Aurelius, is either irrational or unjust.

3. If he were intelligent he would see the worthlessness of his arguments. If he were honest, he would own himself in the wrong. But either he does not see that his arguments are worthless: or seeing that they are he will not own himself in the wrong. Either he is wanting in intelligence, or he is dishonest.

4. If I remain in school I must curtail my expenses, and if I remain in school I must also borrow money. But I find that I can neither curtail my expenses nor borrow money for sufficient funds. Therefore, I cannot remain in school.

5. If I win this case, I must impeach the testimony of one of the witnesses and if I win the case I must induce the judge to give certain instructions to the jury. Either I cannot impeach the testimony of the witness or I cannot induce the judge to give the needed instructions to the jury. Therefore, I shall lose the case.

6. If I plead guilty, I lose the chance of being acquitted, but have the hope of leniency from the court; if I plead not guilty, I take the chance of conviction with no hope of leniency from the court. But, I must either plead guilty or not guilty. Therefore, I must either lose the chance of being acquitted and may hope for leniency from the court, or I must take the chance of conviction without hope of clemency.

7. Either you still have a long life before you or a short one. If a long life, you will forego countless pleasures by devoting yourself exclusively to a religious life; if a short life, you can not get far on the path of holiness

which a religious life demands. Therefore, it is useless to devote oneself exclusively to a religious life.

8. If an officer does his duty, he will obey orders; and if he is intelligent, he will understand them. But this officer either disobeyed his orders or else he misunderstood them. Therefore, he either did not do his duty; or else he is not intelligent.

9. Protagoras, the sophist, agreed to teach Eualthus law on condition that the latter pay for his instruction, when he should have won his first case. Eualthus finished his course under Protagoras; was licensed by the state to practice law, but took up a business career instead, and so never attempted to win a law case. Protagoras brought suit against Eualthus for his promised fee and naturally, Eualthus acted as his own lawyer.

Protagoras argued: Most honorable judge, this young man must pay me my fee. If he loses this suit, he must pay me by order of the court; if he wins this suit he must pay me by the terms of our contract.

To this argument Eualthus answered: Most honorable judge, my worthy opponent has no argument at all. If I lose this suit, I am not yet bound by the terms of my contract with him; if I win the suit, I am absolved from it by the decision of the court.

Did Protagoras have any chance of getting his fee?

*   *   *   *

Complete the following into dilemmas, and then answer them.*

1. If a woman is like man, and it is right for man to vote, it must be right for women to do so. If woman is unlike

---

*In constructing your dilemmas be sure to construct them in the strict logical form for a dilemma. Make certain, especially in a complex constructive dilemma, that your conclusion is disjunctive in form.

man, he can never truly represent her, and she ought to be allowed to represent herself.

2. If Mr. Rhodes knew of Dr. Johnson's raid, he was guilty of complicity; if he did not, of negligence.

3. If a statesman who sees his former opinion to be wrong, does not alter his course, he is guilty of deceit; if he does alter his course, he is open to the charge of inconsistency.

4. It is certain that you are destined either to pass or to fail. Why study?

5. What is the use of worrying whether we act justly or unjustly? If we act justly, we shall displease our friends nearly every time; if we act unjustly, we shall displease God. So there you are.

6. Why should we fear death? As Socrates said, it is either the end of all or it is the beginning of a happy life.

CHAPTER VIII

FALLACIES

Purpose of Logic.—In general, it may be said that the purpose of Logic is to train the mind in such a way as to render it secure against fallacies, for in its widest sense a fallacy is any false process of reasoning.

Definition of a Fallacy.—In the widest sense any false opinion, inaccurate statement, any confusion of ideas, any clumsy expression, any violation of a logical principle is a fallacy. Fallacies are the "wolves in sheep's clothing" of Logic. In the stricter sense, fallacies are arguments which while apparently valid really violate some logical principle concerning the process of thought or concerning the objective logical truth of our thought.

Principal Kinds of Fallacies.—Without claiming to give a complete classification of the ways in which we may arrive at error when we think, we shall attempt to set down here the more common fallacies against which logicians warn us.

Fallacies Divided Into Three Groups. — Broadly speaking, fallacies may be divided into:—(1) Fallacies of language; (2) Logical fallacies; (3) Material fallacies.

FALLACIES OF LANGUAGE

Equivocation.—Equivocation is the fallacy which arises from the use of the same word in different senses in different parts of an argument. In any particular instance of written speech, the context will determine the appropriate sense of an equivocal word. Equivocation covers the case of words which are used analogously as well as those which are purely equivocal. Amphibology is the same fallacy as equivocation except that here the error is due to the doubtful meaning of some phrase instead of one ambiguous word.

Composition and Division.—Composition is the fallacy which consists in taking collectively what ought to be taken separately. Division is the fallacy which consists in taking separately what ought to be taken collectively.

Accent.—The fallacy of 'accent' consists in transferring the stress or accent from one syllable of a word to another, or from one word in a phrase or in a sentence to another word of the phrase or sentence. For instance, which word did Lady Macbeth stress, when she replied, "We fail," to Macbeth's question in reference to the murder of Duncan, "What if we fail?"

LOGICAL FALLACIES

Purely Logical Fallacies.—Purely logical fallacies are those which consist in the violation of any of the laws which regulate the processes of form or validity. Any violation of the rules of the syllogism, for instance, is a purely logical fallacy.

Semi-Logical Fallacies.—Semi-logical fallacies arise from the misunderstanding of one of the terms in an argument, usually the middle term. It is not just the same as equivocation and yet it is partly dependent on words. The two types of semi-logical fallacies are:— (1) fallacy of accident; (2) confusion of the absolute and the qualified statement.

The 'fallacy of accident' assumes two forms: (a) The 'fallacy' of accident occurs whenever we confuse the essential with the accidental attributes of an object; (b) The 'fallacy of accident' occurs, whenever we condemn the use of a thing from the abuse of the same. Man is risible; Risible is a property; Therefore, man is a property,—is an example of confusing the accidental with the essential attributes of man,—Wine is an intoxicant; therefore, it is not lawful to drink wine,—is an example of condemning the use of a thing on account of its abuse.

The fallacy of the 'absolute and qualified statement' occurs when we fail to discriminate between an unqualified statement and one that should be qualified by some restriction, e.g., "It is unlawful to take another's life" is true, only when "to take another's life" is qualified by the word, 'unjustly.'

MATERIAL FALLACIES

What Are Material Fallacies?—Material fallacies are those which occor on account of the content of the argument. They do not arise form the language nor from the process of logic employed, but from the meaning and intent of the argument.

Petitio Principii.—This fallacy called in English, 'begging the question,' consists in taking for granted just the thing we have to prove,—either the whole of what is contended for, or part of it, e.g., Every reputable scientist now-a-days believes in the fact of Evolution. That Evolution is a fact has still to be proved, as well as that every reputable scientist of the present day really does believe it to be a fact.

Ignoratio Elenchi.—An 'ignoratio elenchi' or an 'irrelevant argument or conclusion' occurs when we evade the point at issue, and instead of proving what we should prove, we try to establish some other which is irrelevant, e.g., Philosophy bakes no bread. Why study it? Answer: Philosophy is not necessarily studied for material gain.

Argumentum Ad Hominem.—The 'argumentum ad hominem' consists in turning aside from the question at issue and directing attention to the personality of one's opponent—generally to abuse him. An 'argumentum ad populum' consists in appealing to the prejudices or passions of our hearers or readers instead of holding to the point at issue. An 'argumentum ad verecundiam' consists in trying to disconcert the opponent by urging the superior weight and dignity of authority which seem to be against him. All of these fallacies are but other forms of 'ignoratio elenchi' or 'irrelevant arguments.'

Another form of this same fallacy somewhat popular at the present day is the tendency to transfer reputation from one field to another. To quote a famous inventor on a point of theology; an energetic business man on a problem of broad statesmanship; or an explorer on a question of social ethics; is to commit this fallacy.

Post Hoc, Ergo Propter Hoc—or False Cause.—This is another common fallacy, which consists in assigning effects to an imaginary cause or to a real thing which is not a cause of the effect in question. Just because one thing happens before another it is not necessarily the cause of the second thing. This fallacy of false cause is likewise understood as the fallacy which consists in attempting to show that certain absurd conclusions follow from our adversary's contention, whereas they follow from entirely different premises. For example: If capital punishment is a deterrent of murder, why not inflict it for theft too? Answer: Capital punishment is not upheld simply as a deterrent of murder, but on the ground that there should be some proportion between the crime and its punishment.

Assumed and Dubious Propositions—Suppressing Facts.—Perhaps the most common fallacies in the literature of the present day are: The 'petitio principii,' in the form of inferring certain conclusions from assumed or dubious premises; and secondly, the suppression of facts, when they do not fit in with the purpose of the theories of the writer.

Durant's Story of Philosophy.—A classical example of this last mentioned fallacy occurs in the recently popular book: "The Story of Philosophy." Apparently, the author of this book does not believe that anything worth while or interesting was done in philosophy during the 2,000 years from Socrates to Spinoza. So the author scuttles the whole business. It is so important to know all about Spinoza and Nietzsche, and Schopenhauer, and William James, and Kant, but so unimportant to know about the philosophers who built the great universities; who fused Greek, Arabian and Catholic thought into that mighty synthesis called Scholasticism; who inspired such poetry as Dante wrote. It is so unimportant to know those philosophers who were the founders of that philosophy on which our Declaration of Independence is based.

Fallacies of the Modern Mind.—In addition to an enumeration of fallacies as they are traditionally given in most texts on Logic, it seems worth while to add the following list without classifying them under the logical species to which they may belong, but under the less scientific classification: fallacies of the modern mind.

In general these fallacies are what we call fallacies of simple inspection:—they are, in effect, 'a priori' fallacies. They are for the most part popular maxims and generalizations which are taken for granted, usually without discussion and therefore without suspicion that the content of what is stated by these maxims or generalizations is at least ambiguous if not always downright erroneous. Here are a few such fallacies:

1. The 'a priori' repudiation of one or more methods of attaining knowledge along with the simultaneous assertion that whatever is not known in an arbitrarily selected way is entirely unknowable. It is in this way that rationalism tries to substantiate its denial of revelation.

2. The habit of confusing what is inexplicable with what is false or absurd.

3. The habit of rejecting as false whatever appears to be inconceivable or simply, unimaginable.

4. Holding it as a principle that ideas correspond to things, —logical to the ontological order. This preconception is one of the chief supports of pantheism.

5. The 'a priori' taking it for granted that man has the right to unrestrained liberty.

6. Man is naturally good. Each man has within him the germs of perfection. These develop spontaneously and simultaneously with the organs of his body. This fallacy supposes a belief in the Philosophy of Rousseau.

7. Any authority which attempts to prevent or direct man's development is not auxiliary but inimical to his liberty.

8. The people is sovereign.

9. All men are equal.

10. The presupposition that Nature always takes the shortest and simplest way to reach an end. This fallacy supposes that we always know which is the shortest and simplest way Nature can choose.

11. Seeing what one wishes to see and not seeing what one does not wish to see.

12. Incomplete induction or enumeration.

13. All energy can be explained in terms of mechanical energy.

14. The confounding of a correlation of facts with the identity of facts. "Cum hoc, ergo ipsum hoc."

15. Historical over-emphasis. This fallacy occurs when a writer stresses the dark side of a character or of a movement in question without giving any credit to the good points of the character or of the movement; when the writer at times, may even deliberately ignore the good

points of a character or movement, or falsely claim there are none such.

16. The dogmatic enunciating of propositions which have never been proved either because the writer considers his own word or the word of others sufficient authority for what he says or writes.

EXAMPLES OF FALLACIES

Name the fallacies in the following examples. State the reason why you name each as you do.

1. You must have met him for you were at the University at the same time.
2. These men are traitors for they oppose the President.
3. In Panama the mosquitoes are large and many of them weigh a pound.
4. All Saxons are Germans; No Belgians are Saxons; No Belgians are Germans.
5. No cat has nine tails; One cat has one more tail than no cat; Therefore, one cat has ten tails.
6. Any student in college would stand higher in his class if he received higher marks; hence if all marks were raised ten per cent, every man would stand nearer the head of his class.
7. The right should be enforced by law. The exercise of suffrage is a right, and should, therefore, be enforced by law.
8. Is a stone a body? Yes. Then is not an animal a body? Yes. Are you an animal? I think so. Therefore, you are a stone, being a body.
9. At the time of the Galveston flood, men worked sixteen hours a day: hence it is absurd to talk of an eight-hour day as a necessity for the working classes.

10. A college education does not pay, for most self-made Americans have succeeded without it.

11. Berkeley's theory of the 'non-existence of matter' is absurd for it is palpably impossible even to place one's foot on the ground without experiencing the resistance of matter.

12. The poor must be oppressed for the rich are accumulating millions.

13. Idiots are not men, for men are rational beings.

14. The argument from design to prove an intelligent Creator must be false because it has been rejected by Kant.

15. Great men have been derided. I am derided. Therefore, my theory ought to be adopted.

16. The receiver of stolen property should be punished. You have received stolen property. Therefore, you should be punished.

17. Good men write good books. This is a good book. Therefore, the writer of the book was a good man.

18. In reply to the gentleman's arguments, I need only say that two years ago, he advocated the very measure which he now opposes.

19. Every book is liable to error. Every book is a human production. Therefore, all human productions are liable to error.

20. Of university professors some are zealous investigators and some good teachers. Oswald is an excellent teacher, and so we may conclude he is not a zealous investigator.

21. I will have no more doctors: I see that all those who died this winter have had doctors.

22. No man should be punished if he is innocent; this man should not be punished; therefore, he is innocent.

23. A miracle is incredible because it contradicts the laws of Nature.

24. He who calls you a man, speaks truly; he who calls you a fool, calls you a man; therefore, he who calls you a fool, speaks truly.

25. This person is very learned and very sociable; hence all learned persons are sociable.

26. The spectra of compound bodies become less complex with heat; but the spectra of the elements do not, since they are not the spectra of compound bodies.

27. No pauper has a vote; Smith is not a pauper; therefore, he has a vote.

28. Our ideas reach no farther than our experience. We have no experience of divine attributes and operations. I need not conclude my syllogism. You can draw the inference yourself. (Hume.)

29. Ghosts exist because all people in all ages have had faith in their existence. We know so little of souls even when they animate our bodies and those of our friends; how then can we say they may not become ghosts after death? Besides there are kindly ghosts as well as evil-minded ones. It will be an incentive to virtue if we know that the souls of our departed dear ones, will in the form of ghosts, hover about us, to watch, guide, and protect us.

30. In the case of persons or books revealing both moral guidance and miraculous performances, the former must be regarded as the sole aspect which furnishes their divine credentials; for since the latter without the former may be the work of the devil rather than of God, miraculous performances can add nothing at all to the character of persons or books as divine witnesses. (Burtt, *Principles and Problems of Right Thinking*, p. 562.)

31. Mr. Charles said that he was certain that the donors gave the property to the institution with a distinct and unanimous understanding as to its future use. The directors who acted for the institution in this transfer must necessarily have had an understanding, either the same as that of the donors, or different. If the understanding of the directors was the same as that of the donors, then they, the former, were unquestionably bound to live up to that understanding. If it was different, then the property was conveyed on a misunderstanding, and every dictate of honour and fair play, would demand the return of the property.

32. If Columbus had never lived, America would still have been discovered; if Newton had never lived, someone else would have discovered the law of gravitation; if Wilberforce had never lived, the slave trade could not have lasted forever; therefore, the world could do without great men.

33. All cold can be expelled by heat; your illness is a cold; therefore it can be expelled by heat.

34. The Duke yet lives that Henry shall subdue.

35. "Thou shalt not bear false witness against thy *neighbor*."

36. "And the Prophet said to his servant: 'Saddle me the ass', and he saddled him."

37. Aio te Aeneade, Romanos vincere posse. (I say to thee O scion of Aeneas you the Romans to conquer are able.)

38. The Bible is inspired for the Church says so; the Church is infallible because the Bible says so.

39. Our school has dropped football, and now the pupils get better grades in their studies.

40. When the City Editor of the Western Herald was reprimanded for writing:—"Half of the lawyers in town are

crooks,"—he apologized to the readers of his paper the
next day, thus:—"I was mistaken in my editorial yesterday . . . half of the lawyers in town are not crooks."
(Cf. *Rules for Sub-Contraries,* p. 58.)

41. If the rule which says: "Contradictory propositions cannot both be true nor can they both be false," is a valid
rule, how can Christ be God? If it is true, as it is, that
"Men are not Gods" it must be false that "Some men are
Gods." This seems logical enough, but the rule should
stand even when this contradictory just stated, is limited
to "Some man is God."

42. Criticize the following paragraphs:

The dawn of character in man, and conscience, when
he first began to appreciate the values of the world within
himself, and to worship less the material world outside,
was sketched vividly yesterday by Dr. James Henry
Breasted in his address at the dedication of the new
Oriental institute at the University of Chicago.

Dr. Breasted defied the claims of those he called the
"old school theologians," who would have it that man's
conscience and character were produced by divine revelation or inspiration.

"It was the outgrowth of man's own social experience,"
the noted archeologist proclaimed, from out of his half a
century of searching in the dead worlds. "It sprang out
of his own soul and no outworn theological doctrine of
inspiration, no conception of a spotlight of Divine Provi-
dence shining exclusively on Palestine, shall despoil man
of this crowning glory of his life on earth, the discovery
of character."

The date of this memorable human achievement was
fixed by Dr. Breasted as 2,000 years before the birth of

Christ, and the place in which it transpired was Egypt, perhaps in the shadows of the great pyramids.

Addressing a few hundred distinguished guests who came to witness the dedication of a buidling which is now the greatest headquarters for ancient research in the entire world, and of which he is the director, Dr. Breasted traced through the ages what he called, "The Rise of Man."

He took man as Darwin pictured him, then found him again in the Stone age and described his crude implements, some of which may be seen in the galleries of the institute's museum halls. Then the scientist took his listeners through the Bronze age, and up into the first great civilizations of the Egyptians. *Chicago Tribune,* Dec. 6, 1931.

43. Since a married woman is not a serf but a citizen, her right to abandon her husband and to decide her own future cannot be questioned. (Attributed to Justice McCardie, *America,* vol. xlvi, no. 17; Jan. 30, 1932.)

*44. The system of philosophy called Dualism must be false because it holds that in the ultimate analysis of being, we arrive at two principles; one material, the other spiritual. Now how is it possible for two principles, the one unextended and the other extended—to act upon each other? Such interaction seems not only impossible, but even inconceivable. Besides any interaction of body and mind, or conversely, of mind and body, would upset the law about the conservation of energy.

---

* Fallacies 44 to 48 inclusive, may be found in substance, if not verbatim, in Paulsen's *Introduction to Philosophy.* For a refutation of these fallacies, the student may be referred to Ryan's *Introduction to Philosophy.*

45. Evolution proves that the development of the mind is completely and at all times, dependent on the development of the body. Why then insist that bodily function is different from mental function?

46. Everything must occur and be explained physically, and everything must be considered and interpreted metaphysically.

From the foregoing statement we must conclude that mechanism,—the philosophy which attempts a construction in the terms of mechanics,—is the only tenable theory, so far as the activities of nature are concerned. Metaphysics may have a place in knowledge but it is only as an interpreter of the results achieved by mechanistic science that we can recognize it.

47. Nature prodigally wastes millions of possible beings in order to bring one to complete development. "A single female fish lays hundreds of thousands of eggs a year." Besides Nature creates without any idea of value and for no intelligible purpose. Witness the vermiform appendix. Moreover, if life had a value we should be able to discover it. Has any vitalist pointed out a complete scheme of the ends to be attained by even one species, to say nothing of all the species of nature as a whole?

48. "The former theory (*Vitalism*) which assumed that animal and plant species owe their origin to an intelligence acting from without, is thereby finally overthrown as a natural historical theory—overthrown not by being refuted but, like every worn-out hypothesis, re moved, by the entrance of its legitimate successor, the better theory."

49. Statistics prove that the number of suicides over any given period rises and falls in any given social ambient

altogether independent of freedom of the will. Now figures do not lie. Who then will say that there is any freedom of the will?

50.   The happiness or welfare of mankind in general is the only worthy end for all our actions. According to Christian Ethics an act is right or wrong accordingly as the Divine Lawgiver decrees an act right or wrong, simply because He wills it so. As Nietzsche says, "This is slave morality."

51.   The history of Ethics seems to prove conclusively that there never existed a system of moral ideas which is innate, authoritative, and which was or is now universally acceptable. What one race or one age considers a virtue, in another clime or time was looked upon as immoral; therefore, it is useless to talk about any absolute standard of morality, or to say the truths of morality are universal and binding on all men, as well as known to them.

52.   The soul idea, even though it were true, is useless. Given the brain, thought, of necessity follows. We add nothing to our understanding of brain processes by saying that beneath these processes, the soul exists as a sort of ground or subject for the same. After all the very concept of the soul is an empty one, nor have we any immediate experience of the soul; its existence is the result of inference. On the other hand, we know from experience what consciousness is. Is it logical to assign a higher grade of reality to the soul than we do to the activities in us which we know by consciousness? Well, if we have a soul, the world also, may possess one.

53.   "Now how is it possible for them (*Catholics*) to give a rational assent to the Church's infallibility unless they have some infallible means to know that she is infallible?

Neither can they infallibly know the infallibility of this means, but by some other; and so on forever, unless they can dig so deep, as to come at length to the rock, that is, to settle all upon something evident of itself, which is not so much as pretended." (Chillingworth's fallacy as quoted by Newman, *Grammar of Assent,* p. 226.)

54.   The origin of man is not known, although scientists generally agree that he has developed by the process of evolution, from some high form of animal. This belief is based upon the close resemblance between the body of man and ape, and receives support from the fact that, in habits and modes of living, some savages are little above animals. (R. S. Tarr, *New Physical Geography,* p. 369.)

CHAPTER IX

CLASSIFICATION AND DIVISION

From the definition of the extension of a term, i.e., the number of individuals to which the idea represented by the term can apply,—we see that wide ranges of things are sometimes included under one term. To be dealt with conveniently these things must be put into groups in some systematic manner, i.e., they must be classified.

Classification.—A classification then, is a systematic arrangement of the things included under one idea or term, by dividing them into groups on the basis of different principles of division. For example:—Schools may be divided into: universities, colleges, high schools and grade schools. This division is made on the basis of the character of the curriculum of studies followed in each school. As a second example we might classify the clergy of the Catholic church into: bishops, priests, deacons, sub-deacons, and those in 'minor orders,' this classication being based on the functions of the different members of the clergy.

Genus-Species.—It is customary to name the term with the larger extension, the one whose extension is being divided into smaller groups, the genus. The smaller groups or subdivisions of a genus, are commonly called the species.

128

In the first example above, the genus is schools; the species are: universities, high schools, colleges and grade schools. In the second example, the genus is: the clergy of the Catholic church; the species are: bishops, priests, deacons, sub-deacons and those in 'minor orders.'

Single Basis of Classification.—Notice that in the two examples of classification, just given, a single basis of classification was used. In the first it was 'the character of the curriculum';—in the second, it was 'function of the clergy.' That there must be 'a single basis of classification' is essential in every instance of it. The basis adopted depends upon the purpose of the classification. Once selected, it must be adhered to, or overlapping of species will result.

Differentia.—Each species must possess a characteristic which is peculiar to it alone. This exclusive characteristic is called the differentia. In the example given above, the exclusive characteristic of each of the several schools under the genus, 'schools,' was the peculiar curriculum of studies proper to each species of school. Broadly speaking, the peculiar curriculum of studies in a university, is a curriculum of studies intended to teach and train its students in the recognized higher professions, like medicine, law. The curriculum of a college purports to be one which gives a cultural or liberal education. The high school's curriculum embraces those studies which are of cultural value also, like the college, but in a less intensive way. Finally, the curriculum of a grade school confines itself to a general course of studies which tradition and experience seem to have proved are essential to all for their common well being in society. For the functions peculiar to the different groups of the clergy of the Catholic church, the Catholic dictionary or any standard dictionary may be consulted.

Division.—Division is the process of separating the extension of a genus into its species,—using the term species here in a wide sense. A classification is the systematic arrangement of the extension of a genus which results from the process of division. To classify a thing then is to assign it to its proper place in a process of division. Sometimes the term 'classification' is used to cover both concepts; 'classification and division.'*

Rules of Division.—(1) The division must be made on a single basis. (2) The entire extension,—the total divided—must be included in the species,—i.e., the dividing members. In other words, the sum of the species or dividing members must be just equal to the genus or the total divided. (3) The species or dividing members must be exclusive, that is with no overlapping. (4) Each step should be proximate to the one preceding it.†

---

* A classification need not stop with one division: it may be carried a step further by subdividing each of the species in such a way that a term may be a species with reference to a larger group just above it of which it is a subdivision, while at the same time it may be a genus with reference to smaller groups below it. Thus a term may be both a genus and a species.

† The use of the word 'division' in the foregoing paragraphs must of course mean 'logical division.' Logical division is that operation of the mind by which we distinguish a thing—any total to be divided,—as belonging to a class,—into various sub-classes, and then arranging them in the natural order of their co-ordination and subordination. A physical division would be the taking asunder of a material object into its various

Important Note.—In the foregoing paragraphs, genus, species and the differentia were considered principally from the standpoint of their use in classification or division. We have regarded them only as far as their nature may be known from the standpoint of extension. A more scientific knowledge of them is revealed to us, if we study them from the standpoint of comprehension.

Species, More Scientifically Defined.—The object of an idea represented by any term except the transcendental idea of 'being' can be resolved into constituent attributes which are always implied in the object. For example:—The object of the idea, 'man' always implies the attributes of at least animality and rationality. These attributes implied in the object of an idea are called 'notes' or 'forms'.

Now the number of these notes or forms which are necessary in the object of an idea in order that the idea may truly represent the essential nature of its object, is what is really meant by species. A species then may be defined as those notes or forms or combination of forms implied in any object of an idea, which truly constitute the whole essence of that object. It will be noted that there may be many individuals that contain the same essential forms or notes, not simply one individual. Hence the idea of species always refers to a class of things.

Genus.—If any one of the essential forms or notes making a species, be found to be part of the essence of

---

physical parts. For example:—The taking asunder of an automobile into its chassis and its various working parts: engine, carburetor, gasoline tank and the rest.

other classes of objects or species, it is called a generic form or note, the idea which represents it is called a generic idea, and the thing which will stand as one for all the individuals represented by the generic idea is called the 'genus.' A 'genus' then is that essential note or form which is common to the essences of two or more species.

Differentia.—Now take two species. They agree in something that is common to the essence of both. This is 'genus'. But they differ in other essentials. All the individuals of one species have an essential form which is not in any of the individuals of the other, and which distinguishes all the individuals of one from all those of the other. This objective form which is in one species as an essential note but not in the other or others is called the differentia or specific difference. For example,—the genius is: animal. The genus embraces the two species: rational animal and irrational animal. Rational and irrational are the differentia or specific difference.

Property.—A property is that one, or more than one of the notes which is implied in the object of an idea, not indeed as being essential to the nature of the thing represented by the idea, but as always connected with the essence and flowing from it, e.g., the power of speech in man;—the power of laughter.

Accident.—An accident is that form, note or attribute which happens to be common to many individuals of a class of objects represented by a specific idea, but common in such a way that it is in no way part of the essence, and not even necessarily connected with the essence, e.g., white or black in regard to a class of men.

Predicables.—Genus, species, differentia, property, and accident are called 'heads of predicables' because whatever we predicate of anything comes under one of these heads.

THE PREDICABLES

The predicate of any affirmative proposition must be an attribute (or group of attributes) which either

(a) Belongs to the essence of the subject; in which case it will express: either

  1. The whole essence of the subject, and then it is the species; or

  2. That part of the essence of the subject which the subject has in common with other classes of things, and then it is the genus; or

  3. That part of the essence of the subject which differentiates the subject from all other classes or things, and then it is the difference; or the predicate must be an attribute which

(b) Does not belong to the essence of the subject; in which case it will be: either

  1. Something necessarily connected with the subject, and then it is a property; or

  2. Something not necessarily connected with the subject, and then it is an accident.

Every predicate must be either species, genus, difference, property, or accident of the subject.

Highest Genus—Lowest Species.—When a genus cannot be considered as a species under a higher genus, it is called the 'highest genus'. When a species under one genus cannot be made a genus with reference to individuals under it; that is when the individuals cannot be classified as species, it is called the 'lowest species.' For example, Substance and man represent a highest genus and a lowest species. We cannot predicate anything higher in the scale of things than substance. The individuals under 'man,' on the other hand, cannot be classified as species, because there is no difference between them, essentially.

Diagram for visualizing 'substance' as the highest genus and 'man' as lowest species.

1—*Highest Genus*	1 SUBSTANCE	
2—*Difference*	Corporeal	Incorporeal *(Spirit)*
3—*Subaltern Genus*	3 BODY	
4—*Difference*	Animate	Inanimate *(Mineral)*
5—*Subaltern Genus*	5 LIVING BODY	
6—*Difference*	Sensible	Insensible *(Vegetable)*
7—*Subaltern Genus*	7 ANIMAL	
8—*Difference*	Rational	Irrational *(A brute beast)*
9—*Lowest Species*	9 MAN	

10—*Varieties* BLACK MAN—AN ESQUIMAUX—A HOTTENTOT

Key For Diagram.—Substance, the highest genus, is divided into: corporeal substance, (left), and incorporeal substances, (right), which are the two species under the genus substance. Each species has a definite class name. For corporeal substances it is, 'a body'—for incorporeal substances it is, 'spirit.' Note how the species expressed in its definite class name is in turn a new genus.

Now, read downward, left only. (Diagram has no more reference to species, 'spirit.')

Taking substance as the highest genus (No. 1) and reading down, (left), we see that each odd number indicates a subaltern genus, while each even number indicates a specific difference, until we come to No. 9, (man), which is not called a subaltern genus but the lowest species, because it is impossible to divide 'man' into lower specific groups. No. 10 indicates that we divide 'man' into groups based on accidental differences, which give us varieties of men but not essential different species of men. (See paragraph on varieties.)

This diagram will likewise be useful in visualizing the analysis of real definitions. If read 'upward' (left) it shows clearly the specific difference and proximate genus of certain terms, e.g., man, animal, a living being, a body;—and read upward, (right), of the terms in italics: brute, vegetable, mineral, spirit.

Varieties.—True it is for purposes of division, the term 'man' could be used as standing for a genus and we could have any number of divisions of men based on some accidental characteristic as a basis for our division; as, black, white men, hump-backed men, etc. Species in this sense, i.e., when it means the differentia-tion of the individuals of some given lowest species on the basis of an accidental characteristic of the individuals, is not species in the scientific meaning of the term, but 'varieties.' In the question of evolution and in the science of biology, great confusion can occur from a failure to understand the difference between 'species' and 'varieties'.

EXERCISES

In the following examples state whether the *italicized* terms are *genus, species, difference, property* or *accident*:
1. An organism is a living *corporeal substance.*
2. A plant is a *corporeal substance.*
3. A man is a being *capable of expressing thought in words.*
4. All men are *rational.*
5. Some policemen are *tall.*

*   *   *   *

In each of the following examples state whether the predicate is *species, genus, difference* or *accident.* Determine whether the correct *proximate genus* is given in each case where a *genus* is given.
1. Animals are beings capable of sensation.
2. An universal concept is an act of the mind by which the mind represents to itself some one thing common to many.
3. Plants are material substances.
4. Some plants are perennial.
5. Some dogs are short-haired.
6. Bodies have extension.
7. A square is a four-sided plane figure.

8. All living things are capable of growth.
9. Alexander the Great was a soldier.
10. Temperance is a virtue which enables us to practice moderation in all things.
11. Money is a measure of value.

*   *   *   *

Examine the following proposed divisions and point out which are logical and which are not:

1. Men into imaginative and unimaginative.
2. Theories into true and false.
3. Schools into technical, preparatory, professional, and scientific.
4. Books into bound and unbound.
5. Soldiers into artillery, cavalry, privates and volunteers.
6. Plants into poisonous and non-poisonous.
7. Women into pretty, silly, and clever.
8. Europeans into peasants, Parisians, Bolsheviks and Catholics.
9. Orchards into those that grow bush-fruit, tree-fruit and vines.
10. Experience into pleasant and painful.
11. Logic into terms, propositions, reasonings, demonstrations and the syllogism.
12. Geometry into plane, solid and spherical.
13. Ideas into clear, distinct and abstract.
14. Plants into root, stalk and leaves.
15. Animals into brutes and men.

CHAPTER X

DEFINITION

"The sophist and the demagogue flourish in an atmosphere of vague and inaccurate definition." (Irving Babbitt—*Democracy and Leadership,* p. 281.)

Nature of Definition.—Definition, in the truest sense of the word, is the statement of the essential constituent elements, notes or forms implicitly contained in the comprehension of any particular object of an idea. When we define a thing, therefore, we set forth in an explicit statement the real nature of the object defined.

A definition which explicitly sets forth the real nature of the object defined is called either, an essential, a logical, a metaphysical definition, or a definition by species.

Unfortunately there are few things we can define by an essential definition. For the most part we have to be content with what is called descriptive definition.

A descriptive definition will enable us to distinguish the object defined from other objects, but it does not tell us wherein it differs from them intrinsically. For this reason a descriptive definition of its very nature must be inadequate from the point of view of Logic.

What is a Descriptive Definition?—A descriptive definition is one which characterizes the object defined
138

by some accidental qualities which serve to identify the object but which do not tell us anything about the intrinsic nature of the object. Descriptive definition is the only way we have of defining individuals. Secondly, descriptive definition includes that class of definitions which identify an object by a description which is extrinsic to the object defined, e.g., by a reference to the use of a thing. An example of a definition by giving the accidental qualities of a thing would be, for instance: A bee is a large insect that makes honey. An example of definition by a description extrinsic to the object defined would be: Tin is a white metal used in roofing and canning.

Distinctive Definitions.—Distinctive definitions are those statements which enable us to identify an object by assigning one or more of its inseparable properties, instead of its differentia. Such definitions are not quite the same as descriptive definitions, as the latter may assign a collection of separable accidents to identify an object. Distinctive definitions are most commonly met with in the physical and natural sciences—chemistry, botany, zoology,—their purpose being to identify the individuals by the possession of certain natural properties.

Nominal Definitions.—Both essential and descriptive definitions are real definitions. This means that both refer to the object of the idea as the thing to be defined, not the term which represents the object. When a definition simply sets forth the etymological force of a term, or when it simply gives the meaning which a term has in everyday use, the definition is called nominal definition.

A real definition attempts to define what the object is which is designated by the term. Technical definitions are those which assign to some terms a definite sense in which they must be understood in any given context.

Physical Definitions.—Physical definitions are nothing more than the description of a physical object by an enumeration of the parts of which it is composed.

Dictionary Definitions.—The so-called definitions to be found in dictionaries belong for the most part to one or other of these classes of substitutes for real essential definitions. They are descriptions, or, at best, distinctive explanations, rather than definitions.

And the same is largely true of what passes as definition in literature, in prose as well as poetry. It is only in scientific works we may hope to find the precision of thought which it is the aim of logical definition to secure.

Rules of Definition.—The following rules give the conditions which a good definition should fulfill, and at the same time the characteristics which serve to distinguish an accurate from a defective definition.

1.   A definition should be exact—it should apply to all of the thing defined and only to the thing defined. For example, A horse is a domestic animal,—this definition does not include the qualities by which horses are distinguished from cows. It might be applied to dogs as well as horses.

2.   A definition should be clear. More specifically, it should be clearer than the thing defined. Thus it would not elighten the average man to be told: The soul is

the first entelechy of the organized body having the potency of life.

3. A definition should not contain the word defined or a derivative from it. For example, A governor is one who governs.

4. A definition should be expressed in literal not in figurative language. Do not define sleep as the brother of death.

5. A definition should be expressed in affirmative language. The number of things which a thing is not is infinite; the number of things which it is, is necessarily restricted.

6. A definition should be brief. No unnecessary words. One of the most common faults of construction in expressing definitions, is to define an object not by a noun but by a subordinate clause. For example, Honesty is 'when one does not steal.'*

A Genetic Definition.—A genetic definition is one that gives us neither the essential nature of the thing nor its properties, but the elements which taken in conjunction, result in its production, i.e., a genetic definition gives the process for producing a thing. It is most frequently used in mathematics, as: A circle is a figure formed by the revolution of a line in a plane around one of its extremities.

Causal Definitions.—Causal definitions are of two kinds—one class defines by indicating the final cause, i.e., the purpose of the thing. For example, A clock is an instrument used to indicate the hours of the day.

---

* In every definition it is always possible to give the correct proximate genus, even though it is not always possible to give the exact 'differentia.'

The other class of causal definitions explains a thing by stating the efficient cause, i.e., that by which something is done.

CRITICIZE THE FOLLOWING EXAMPLES OF DEFINITIONS:

1. "Life is the definite combination of heterogeneous changes, both simultaneous and successive, in correspondence with external co-existences and sequences."— Herbert Spencer. *clear*

2. "Life is the continuous adjustment of internal relations to external relations."—Herbert Spencer. *clear*

3. Money is a measure of value. *fig*

4. A parallelogram is a four-sided figure whose opposite sides are parallel and equal. *generic*

5. A circle is a curve generated by one extremity of a straight line revolving in a plane around the other extremity fixed. *generic*

6. An equilateral triangle is a triangle having three equal sides and three angles. *too wide*

7. Tin is a metal lighter than gold.

8. A laborer is one who performs manual work for wages.

9. A net is a reticulated fabric, decussated at regular intervals, with interstices and intersections. *clear*

10. Injustice is when one does not keep a covenant. *affirm*

11. Bread is the staff of life. *fig*

12. An archbishop is one who exercises archiepiscopal functions. *def*

13. A point is that which has neither length, breadth, nor thickness. *gen*

14. A star is a stellar body seen in the heavens at night. *def*

15. A stool is a single seat without a back.

16. A citizen of this country is one who is not an alien; and an alien is one who is not a citizen.

17. A centaur means a being half man and half horse.

18. Oats is a grain which in England is generally given to horses, but in Scotland supports the people.

19. A clock is a mechanical instrument to indicate the time.

20. Friendship is the link which binds together two hearts into one.

21. Life is the opposite of death.

22. A phonograph is a mechanism for recording and reproducing sounds.

23. The body is the emblem or visible garment of the soul.

24. Psychology is the science of the phenomena of consciousness.

25. Education is conscious or voluntary evolution.

26. Religion consists in the feeling of absolute dependence.

27. Religion is a desire manifested by prayer, sacrifice and faith.

28. Religion is a faculty of the mind by which independently of the senses and of reason, man is able to perceive the Infinite.

EXERCISES IN DEFINITION

Define the following terms. Determine the nature of each definition given. Is your definition an essential or specific definition? descriptive? distinctive? genetic or causal?

sociology	tort	moratorium
corporation	tariff	communism
primaries	anarchy	fascism
edema	triangle	bolshevism
mechanism	dogma	metaphysics
ballad	rhombus	

CHAPTER XI

ANALOGY

Nature of Analogy.—Loosely used, the term 'analogy' stands for any mark of similarity or resemblance which enables us to reason from one thing to another. Analogy then, may be defined as inference based on resemblance.

The resemblance referred to may be between two things or persons or it may be a likeness between certain relations. For instance there is a likeness between a king or ruler and a captain of a football team; or between an army and a football team. There is likewise a resemblance or relation between a bishop and his diocese, with the relation of a shepherd to his sheepfold. Again there is a similarity of relationship between the citizens of a state and the established government in the state, comparable in some way to the relationship of the different members of the body with the body itself.

This is all very well, but we must always pause before making an inference from analogy to find out if there be differences as well as resemblances between the persons, things or relations. We must cautiously check any too hasty tendency to regard resemblances even as a probable sign of further resemblances between the terms of an analogy. Just because two twins are alike in looks, height, color, color of hair and so on, and then, just because one of the twins has a birthmark on his

left shoulder, it does not follow that the other has one
on the same part of his body.

Analogy Gives Only Probable Conclusion.—The
most striking feature of analogical reasoning is found in
the fact that it yields only probable conclusions. The
reason for this is that analogy is a method of reasoning
from one particular to another on the basis of some
imagined or perceived similarity between the two cases.
Complete logical certainty, however, is attained only
when the new fact or group of facts is really and essentially united by means of some general principle with
what is already known. There is no genuine inference from particular to particular; inference proceeds
through a universal.

But although argument from analogy yields only
probable conclusions, probability is not a fixed quantity.
An argument from analogy may have degrees of value
from zero almost up to the limit of complete logical
certainty.

Value of Analogy.—The value of an analogical
argument will depend on the nature of the resemblance
which is taken as the basis of inference. In general, it
is true that the greater the number of resemblances, the
more certainly we can reason from one thing to another.
This is not to say, however, that the value of the conclusion is in direct proportion to the number of points
of resemblance which can be discovered. We must
weigh points of resemblance rather than count them;
they must represent some deep-lying characteristic of
the things concerned. For example, we might argue:
John and James are the same height, live in the same

house, come from the same town, formerly went to the same school; John stands high in his class; therefore, James probably does also. If the number of points in this example were the essential thing, the argument ought to possess some weight, but it is clear that it has none. If we knew that the two boys were similar in character, this one similarity would be worth more as a basis for our conclusion than all the other circumstances or similarities enumerated in the example, combined.

Reasoning from analogy is reducible to a syllogism thus: Similar things have similar properties, e.g., similar causes, effects, purposes; but A and B are similar things; therefore, they have similar properties. A has the property X; therefore, B has the same property.

Why Analogy is Used.—Since analogical reasoning can furnish no conclusive assurance of validity, the question is quite naturally raised as to why it should be so much used. The answer is: analogy serves as a basis for hypotheses. Hypotheses are guesses held tentatively in the mind while they are tested. We draw working hypotheses from analogous experiences by means of analogous reasoning.

Testing Hypotheses.—Notice that in the definition of an hypothesis, above, it was stated that an hypothesis is a guess held tentatively in the mind while the guess is tested. Herein is the value of analogy. We see a certain likeness between two things. We know all about one of the things—its cause, purpose, effects; of the other thing we know nothing, but we see some resemblance between it and the thing we do know. Therefore, our conclusion is that the unfamiliar thing must be the same as the thing which we do know, e.g., in cause, purpose, effects. At this point we must not hastily conclude as stated before, but test. Test for what? To see whether the reason for the likeness between the two things is merely accidental or whether it is fundamental and essential. If we find that the likeness between the two things is fundamental and essential to the real nature of the things compared, we have made analogy serve its one useful purpose; we can go now beyond the 'tentative' stage to certitude; instead of inferring only a probable conclusion we can now reach a true and valid one. The reason is this: If a property is shown to be not merely accidental to an individual but a constant and uniform property of the nature to which the individual belongs, it will be a property not only to this particular individual but to all the individuals of the same nature, because nature is uniform in essential and fundamental properties.

A Warning.—Great care must be taken when testing analogous argument not to mistake an accidental for an essential, fundamental constituent element or for a necessary concomitant property of any particular individual or class of things. It is likewise easy to mistake a condition or an occasion for a real cause. For instance light is a condition, a sine-qua-non for reading these pages but it is in no way an efficient or any other kind of a cause for my reading them. In the same way, tails are not a necessary concomitant property to monkeys, horses or to other animals. The ordinary untutored and undisciplined mind is led astray by striking external and accidental resemblances,—by the fallacies of figurative and analogical language. A trained mind will penetrate beneath the surface and apprehend the real fundamental resemblance. It will see beyond the chaos of particular facts, and detect the underlying principle by means of which these particular facts can be connected and systematized. It is only in this way that analogy passes from the stage of a mere argument from particular to particular, to the perception of a general law which includes the individual instances. But no such direct insight can claim the title of knowledge until it is tried and tested by facts. The guesses of many men at times, unfortunately, have proved to be mistakes.

Conclusion.—To fully explain or prove any fact, we are obliged to go beyond analogy and verify its conclusions by bringing them into relation to a general principle.

EXAMPLES OF ANALOGY

Discuss the following arguments from analogy. Determine the value of each:

1. According to Carlyle, a representative form of government is bound to fail, since as he put it, a ship could never be taken around Cape Horn if the captain were obliged to consult the crew every time before changing the course.

2. Just as the different members are subservient to the good of the whole body, so individual citizens are entirely subservient to the State.

3. The Earth and Mars are alike in several respects: both are planets: both revolve around the Sun: both turn on their axes: both have an atmosphere and a change of seasons. The Earth is inhabited. Therefore, Mars is likewise inhabited.

4. These two automobiles are Franklins. They must have the same number of cylinders.

5. Smith's apartment in Hyde Park paid him twenty per cent profit last year. His apartment was a duplex just like yours.

6. Caesar had his Brutus. It is easy to see what will happen to those who ambition power.

7. War is a blessing. Show me the nation that has ever become great without bloodletting.

8. Italy is a Catholic country and abounds in beggars. Ireland is also a Catholic country. Therefore, there must be a lot of beggars in Ireland.

9. If a congressman is 'the hired man' of his constituents he ought to be controlled in casting his vote upon measures in which his constituents are interested, by their judgment, not by his own.

10. It is silly to talk about the United States giving the Filipinos their independence, just as it would be for parents to let their chidlren go uncared for or uncontrolled before they reach the age of discretion.

11. Thousands are ruined and thousands are killed by the automobile every year. To be consistent prohibitionists ought to work for a law prohibiting autos. In the same way many other people ruin their stomachs with pickles and other condiments. I wonder why prohibitionists don't shout for a law against these articles of food.

CHAPTER XII

INDUCTION

Deduction vs. Induction.—Deduction is that form of reasoning which proceeds from a general principle or a universal law to the conclusion of a particular fact. Induction is that form of reasoning which proceeds from particular facts and arrives at a conclusion which is a general statement of a universal law.

Induction starts where observation has furnished it a starting point. Observation seeks facts as such and records their presence and their nature. Induction is thinking from these known facts on to a general principle.

Purpose of Induction.—The purpose of induction is the derivation of universal laws embracing under their sway a great number of facts.

Perfect Induction.—Now it should be kept in mind that induction is a form of inference and not merely a substitution of a general statement for several individual statements embraced under it. Such a summary statement, it is true, is called perfect or complete induction, but in truth, it is not induction at all. Perfect induction consists merely of the observation that each and every individual of a class, possesses a certain characteristic, and then the assertion that all the individuals of the class possess it. There is nothing at all new in such an assertion; there is merely a general statement embracing as many individual statements as there are individuals in the class. For example, When a jury of twelve men has been polled and one after the other from the first to the twelfth, votes for the verdict, there is no inference involved in passing from these twelve facts to the general statement: All the members of the jury favor the verdict.

Such induction as just exemplified in the preceding example, is, as was stated, called perfect induction or complete enumerative induction. Even when enumerative induction is complete it may be of little scientific value, because it assigns no cause. It may nevertheless lead to the discovery of a cause. For example, If I discover that all the books in a certain library are books on science, this fact may lead me to discover that the owner of the library is a scientist.

Enumerative Induction.—When it is incomplete, enumerative induction gives only a probable conclusion, not a certitude. The probability is greater as the enumeration nears completeness.

Scientific Induction.—Scientific or causal induction is the real induction. It gives certitude. What then is scientific induction? It is a process of reasoning by which from comparatively few observed facts or cases we discover laws or principles that govern the phenomena or activities of the material world.

Scientific induction comprises the following steps:

Observation.—Observation of facts is the first step, in inductive reasoning. Certain facts or phenomena presented to the senses are observed. These facts may become known either by observation of events in the course of natural occurrences, or by the observation of what happens as the result of artificially arranged experiments. For example, Several persons at the same banquet are temporarily poisoned. This is an observed fact. It serves as a starting point for the investigation of its cause by the inductive process.

Hypothesis.—The supposed cause of the fact of our observation is an hypothesis. After the fact is observed, we naturally ask: How did it happen? What was its cause? The human mind naturally seeks the cause of observed phenomena. For example, Every one poisoned at this particular banquet had eaten besides other food, 'lobster.' It may have been tainted. We then suppose that the tainted lobster may have been the cause. So far, however, the cause selected is only tentative— a clever guess. It is an hypothesis. An hypothesis again, therefore, is a supposed cause of a phenomenon, provisionally selected with a view of eventually ascertaining the true cause of the phenomenon in question.

We must be careful not to make the mistake of accepting the hypothesis of the supposed cause as the real, certain cause of the phenomenon which it professes to explain. At best, so far, the only conclusion we may validly draw from the example about tainted lobster is: Tainted lobster may possibly be the cause.

An hypothesis to be admissible as an hypothesis at all must be: (a) Possible; (b) It must be able to explain all the main facts of experience in the case; (c) It must not either in itself or in its consequences contradict any other certainty, known fact or law.

Verification.—The third step in induction is verification. It is that process by which the investigator tests whether the supposed cause, or the hypothesis, is the real, true cause of the phenomenon under consideration. For example, Was tainted lobster the real, true cause of the poisoning of the guests at the banquet? To find this out, the investigator will continue to try to discover whether some other cause besides tainted lobster might not have played a part in causing the poisoning. Therefore: (a) Every other possible cause must be eliminated; (b) By deduction, conclusions will be drawn from the chosen hypothesis, and observations made as to whether the conclusions drawn, agree in other cases with the facts of Nature; (c) Investigations should be continued until the investigator is convinced that the supposed cause is the only necessitating cause of the phenomenon. Verification is the kernel of the whole process of induction.

Generalization.—After we are convinced that the supposed cause or the hypothesis we have selected as the cause of any particular fact, is the true cause of that fact, it is rational to assume that the same phenomenon or fact will occur whenever and wherever the same cause is present. For example, Tainted lobster will always cause poisoning. This constant way of action is inherent in the causal agency and it is called the law of the uniformity of nature. This law in itself is not self-evident, like the law of causation, i.e., nothing happens without a cause—but it finds its ultimate explanation in the reason and will of an all-wise and omnipotent Ruler of the universe.

Justification of Induction.—Why then from the observation of a few particular facts can we proceed to the assertion of a universal law? The justification of the mental process certainly does not rest upon experience itself. Experience as per supposition extends to only a few cases. Hence, empiricists and positivists who teach that all knowledge is due to experience, utterly fail to justify their own pet form of reasoning—induction. The ultimate justification of the law of the uniformity of nature rests on the reason and will of an all-wise Creator who has endowed all physical agencies with regular constant modes of activity.

METHODS OF VERIFICATION IN SCIENTIFIC INDUCTION (Mill.)

The Method of Agreement.—When a phenomenon has occurred in several different cases and these several different cases have a single circumstance in common, this common circumstance is probably the sufficient reason or cause of the phenomenon. For example, Several persons eat oysters at the same meal and all are poisoned. The oysters were probably the cause of the poisoning.

The Method of Difference.—If an instance in which the phenomenon under investigation occurs and an instance in which it does not occur have every circumstance in common save one, and this particular one occurring only in the former; the circumstances in which alone the two instances differ is the effect or cause, or at least an indispensable part of the cause of the phenomenon. For example, A bell is rung in a jar containing air. The sound is heard. The air is removed. The bell is again struck. The sound is not heard. We conclude that the air is the cause of transmitting the sound.

The Method of Remainders or Residue.—Eliminate from any phenomenon such part of it as is known by previous inductions to be the effect of certain antecedent causes and the remainder or residue of the phenomenon is the effect of the remaining antecedents. For example, My lamp has been lighted for two hours. The temperature of my room has risen from 65 to 70 degrees. How do you explain the additonal five degrees? The increase in heat is due to the lamp and my body. There is no fire. The lamp is now burned for the same length of time while the room is unoccupied. The temperature shows an increase of four degrees. I conclude that my body was the cause of the additonal one degree.

The Method of Concomitant Variations.—That phenomenon which varies in any manner whenever another phenomenon varies in some particular manner, is either a cause or an effect of that phenomenon or is connected with it through some fact of causation. For example, Instead of striking a bell in a complete vacuum, we can strike it with just a little air in the receiver of the air-pump. We then hear a faint sound. Increase the air and the sound increases. This shows that the air is the cause of the transmission of sound.

EXAMPLES OF INDUCTIVE ARGUMENTS

Analyze the examples of inductive reasoning below and point out what methods are employed. Indicate whether or not the con-

clusion is completely established, and name the fallacy, if any,
present:

1. Beeswax, gum-arabic and balsam all take on the brilliant
   coloring of mother of pearl when they receive an impress
   from its surface. The only circumstance in common is the
   shape of the mother of pearl. The shape, therefore, is
   the cause of the brilliant coloring.

2. Overdriven cattle, if killed before recovery from their
   fatigue, become rigid and putrefy in a surprisingly short
   time. A similar fact has been observed in the case of
   animals hunted to death, cocks killed during or shortly
   after a fight, and soldiers slain in battle. These cases
   agree in no circumstances directly connected with the
   muscles except that these have just been subjected to
   exhausting exercises.

3. When a man is shot through the heart, we know that it
   is a gunshot which killed him, supposing that he was
   in the fulness of life immediately before the shooting?

4. What method of verification did Pascal employ when he
   established the causal connection between the height of a
   column of mercury in a tube and the weight of the atmosphere?

5. Some statisticians maintain that the criminal records show
   an increase of murder in countries where capital punishment has been abandoned, and no corresponding increase
   in countries where it is still maintained. If these facts are
   as represented, one is forced to conclude that capital
   punishment tends to diminish the number of murders.

6. Protestant historians sometimes maintain that wherever
   the Catholic Church has held sway, illiteracy prevails,
   and that wherever the influence of the Church is dimin-

ished, education flourishes. Therefore, the Catholic Church has a deleterious influence on education.

7. Wages in the United States are higher than in England because the United States is a republic and has a protective tariff.

8. A unique phenomenon of coloration in the sky occurred in 1883. In the same year a tremendous volcanic explosion occurred in the Straits of Sunda, and that also was of unique intensity. The coincidence of the two, led to the belief that the one was caused by the other.

9 .Why does blood clot when out of the body, and why does it not clot while it remains within the blood-vessels? The accepted explanation until the middle of the eighteenth century was that the clotting was due to cold and rest. In 1767, William Hawson put this explanation to a crucial test. He ligatured a vein in the neck of a dog in two places and then covered it with the skin to prevent its cooling. Opening the vein after an interval, he found the blood in it coagulated.

10. A buttercup leaf, a blade of grass, a fern, a moss, a volvox; all contain green coloring matter. I infer that all the members of the vegetable kingdom contain green coloring matter.

11. Manufacturing countries are always rich countries; countries that produce raw materials are always poor; therefore, if we would be rich we must have manufactures and in order to get them we must encourage them.

12. All cities have theaters, and the more they have the larger the city. Look at New York. Chicago ranks next to New York in wealth and population.

13. It has been found that linnets when shut up and trained with singing larks—the skylark, woodlark, or titlark—

will adhere entirely to the songs of these larks instead of the natural song of the linnets. We may infer, therefore, that birds learn to sing by imitation and that their songs are no more innate than language is in men.

14. We observe very frequently that very poor handwriting characterizes the manuscript of able men, while the best handwriting is as frequent with those who do little mental work when compared with those whose penmanship is poor. We may infer, therefore, that poor penmanship is caused by the influence of severe mental labor.

INDEX

'A' propositions, meaning of, 146.

Absolute vs. qualified statement, fallacy of, 114.

Abstract ideas, 31; terms, 31; what part of speech are abstract terms? 31

Accent, fallacy of, 113.

Accident, definition of, 132-133; fallacy of, 114.

Acts, cognitive of the mind, 15.

Added determinants, 70; rules for, 71; ex. on, 78.

Adjectives, as concrete terms, 31; no extension to, 37; quantifying, 36-37.

Affirmative propositions; 'A' propositions, 45; particular or 'I' propositions, 47.

Aim, of Logic, 17.

Agreement, and difference, method of, 154.

'America', 124.

Amphibology, fallacy of, 113.

Analogous use of terms, 32; explanation of, 33.

Analogy, definition of, 144; only probable conclusions from, 145; value of, 145; why used, 146; warning about, 147; conclusion about, 148.

Analysis of categorical propositions, 43-44.

Answer, how to, a dilemma, 104.

Antecedent, definition of, in conditional propositions, 52-53.

'A Posteriori' propositions, 49.

'A priori' propositions, 49

Apprehension, simple, definition of, 15.

Argument, valid, definition of, 20, good, definition of, 21, 25, under Important Note.

Argumentum, ad hominem, ad populum, ad verecundiam, 115.

Aristotle, 1-2; dictum de ommi et nullo, of, 81.

Aristotelian sorites, definition of, 86; analyses of, 86; example of, 87.

Assumed and dubious proposition, fallacy of, 116.

Babbit, Irving, *Democracy and Leadership,* quotation from, 138.

Basis of classification, single, 129.

Being, nature of, 28; different kinds of, 29, 30; beings of the mind, 15; exercise on distinguishing the different kinds of being, 38-39.

Begging the Question, fallacy of, 115.

Blackmar and Gillen, *Outline of Logic,* quotation from, 11.

Breasted, Dr. James Henry, address, quotation from, 123.

Burtt, *Principles and Problems of Right Thinking,* quotation from, 121.

Causal definition, kinds of, 141-142.

Categorematic terms, 31.

Categorical propositions, 41; reading or analyses of, 43.

Chillingworth's *Fallacy,* 127.

Classification, definition of, 128; single basis of, 129; of ideas, 31, 32.

Clear idea, definition of, 32.

Cognitive acts of the mind, 15.

Collective terms, 36.

Composed on the Intertype in Garamond, and printed from original plates by the Marquette University Press, Milwaukee, Wisconsin. Bound by the Boehm Bindery Company, Milwaukee, Wisconsin. Paper Manufactured by the S. D. Warren Company, Boston, Massachusetts. Fifth printing.